Echoes from an Empty Sky

Echoes from an Empty Sky

THE ORIGINS OF THE BUDDHIST DOCTRINE OF THE TWO TRUTHS

John B. Buescher

SNOW LION
BOULDER

Snow Lion
An imprint of Shambhala Publications, Inc.
4720 Walnut Street
Boulder, Colorado 80301
www.shambhala.com

Printed in the United States of America

♾ This edition is printed on acid-free paper that meets the American National Standards Institute Z39.48 Standard.
♻ Shambhala Publications makes every effort to print on recycled paper. For more information please visit www.shambhala.com.

Distributed in the United States by Penguin Random House LLC and in Canada by Random House of Canada Ltd

Text designed and typeset by Gopa & Ted2, Inc.

The Library of Congress Cataloguing-in-Publication Data
Buescher, John B. (John Benedict)
Echoes from an empty sky: the origins of the Buddhist doctrine of the two truths/John B. Buescher.
p. cm.
Includes bibliographical references.
ISBN 978-1-55939-220-4 (alk. paper)
1. Truth—Religious aspects—Buddhism. 2. Buddhism—Doctrines. I. Title.
BQ4255.B84 2005
294.3'42—dc22
2004028508

Contents

Introduction

Buddhists long ago developed a doctrine of two truths—conventional truth and ultimate truth. They have understood this doctrine in two ways. The first—which appears to have been its original meaning—referred to the sorts of true statements that the Buddha made: his "worldly," sometimes ambiguous, conventional discourse, and his statements or discourse that plainly referred to the ultimate truth. The second way referred to the sorts of objects in the world.

The first way to understand this doctrine dealt with problems Buddhists encountered in their exegesis of the scriptures, particularly in abstracting the Buddha's highest teachings from the mass of his discourses. Each of the many early schools of Buddhism used the doctrine in internecine debates to distinguish what it saw as the Buddha's highest teachings from what it believed other schools had mistaken as ultimate truths, or had invented altogether. In this sense, the doctrine covered much of the same ground as another early distinction—between scriptures that were literal or definitive, and those that were figurative or required interpretation.

This early development of the doctrine of two truths is traced here briefly. Some is excavated from fragmentary evidence of the scriptures of the early schools, and most particularly in the scriptures and commentaries of the Pali canon, which preserve the traditions of the Theravāda School, a close descendant of one of these early Indian schools, the Sthaviravāda.

The second way that Buddhists have understood the doctrine of two truths was as categories of all the objects in the universe or as the modes of objective reality. Treating the doctrine of two truths this way, however, moved the Buddhists' internal debates about the status of scriptures and statements away from the doctrine of two truths (now seen as categories of objective phenomena), and framed them as debates about which scriptures or statements needed interpretation and which did not. This was how matters stood in the period after the earliest proliferation of schools, that is, the period of early classical Indian Buddhism, depicted in the Tibetan Buddhist histories as comprising four major schools—the two Hīnayāna schools of the Vaibhāṣika (or Sarvāstivāda) and the Sautrāntika and the two Mahāyāna schools of the Cittamātra (or Yogācāra) and the Mādhyamika.

Who was most responsible for shifting the doctrine of two truths from a way to talk about scripture to a way to talk about the objective world is not clear, although it may have been the result of efforts to distill lists of the most important things discussed in the discourses (*sūtra*) of the Buddha's *dharma* ("teachings"). These lists were the essentials of the teachings of the *dharma* and so were the *abhidharma* ("higher teachings"). The Hīnayāna Vaibhāṣika School developed what it regarded as comprehensive lists of ultimate "truths"—that is, objects that ultimately existed, as distinguished from those that existed merely conventionally. They practiced their analytical skills—otherwise applied to distinguishing reliable statements or scriptures from unreliable ones—to an exacting, detailed elaboration of what exists. Nevertheless, the schools of this classical Indian period of Buddhism regarded the doctrine of the two truths in this way, as referring to two classes of objects in the universe. Debates between the schools about the nature of reality were conducted in terms of distinguishing objects in the universe that existed conventionally from those that existed ultimately. Or, to put it in other words, which objects were in the class of "conventional truths" and which were "ultimate truths."

The Vaibhāṣikas' doctrine of two truths involved an elaborate atomic theory because the distinction they drew between the conventional and the ultimate was between compounds and simples. They argued that compounded objects were not ultimately real, even though they had a conventional reality. Their goal was to specify the objects that were elemental and so were ultimate "truths" in the sense that they were not susceptible to further analysis.

Their elaborate effort to specify these ultimate simples was important for the development of the discipline of philosophical analysis. But another effect they could not have anticipated or wished for was that their analysis of the objects of the world—their *abhidharma*—was the touchstone for the great protest that eventually identified itself as the Mahāyāna (the "great vehicle"), placing the Vaibhāṣikas with their analysis of the *abhidharma* in the Hīnayāna (the "little vehicle"). The Perfection of Wisdom (*prajñā-pāramitā*) literature, beginning about the first century C.E., mounted an assault on the detailed lists of the Vaibhāṣikas' class of ultimate truths. All of the truths that the Vaibhāṣika *abhidharma* regarded as ultimate—that is, as incapable of further division—were shown to be no such thing. They were, in reality, compounds, or were conditioned, or, we might say, defined not in themselves but only by their causes, conditions, or contexts. All the ultimate truths of the Hīnayāna were dissolved in the Perfection of Wisdom, and were therefore shown to be mere conventional truths. What then, according to the Mahāyāna analysis, was an ultimate truth? It was a conventional truth's emptiness of being what it was in and of itself—it was incapable of withstanding such analysis.

This marked the major divide within Buddhism, in its historical development and among the various schools. The doctrine of the two truths—conventional and ultimate—became, for the Mahāyāna, and especially the Mādhyamika School within it, the essence of the Buddha's teaching, which revealed the nature of the world and all things in it. Understanding that doctrine constituted enlightenment, and the achievement of nirvāṇa. The Mādhyamikas viewed the entire body of Buddhist teachings through the spectacles of the doctrine of the two truths. The Tibetan scholastic schools inherited the Mādhyamika viewpoint from their Indian Buddhist teachers and preserved the sources for studying it. They also developed their own commentaries on these sources.

The heart of this book is a translation of a portion of a Tibetan text on the subject of the two truths. The text is Ngawang Belden's (Ngag-dbang dPal-ldan, b. 1797) *An Explanation of the Meaning of the Conventional and the Ultimate in the Four Tenet Systems (Grub mtha'i bzhi'i lugs kyi kun rdzob dang don dam pa'i don rnam par bshad pa legs bshad dpyid kyi dpal mo'i glu dbyangs)*, which he wrote in 1835 in Urga, Mongolia. The first section of his book is a compendium of views on the doctrine of the two truths in the first of the four "tenet systems" (as the Tibetans classify them), the Vaibhāṣika system. One might wonder how valuable it might be to study the "lowest" of the systems on the subject that is of most importance to the "highest." But the Mahāyāna's central doctrine of emptiness—expressed in the teaching of the two truths—precipitated, as it were, out of the storm clouds of disputes within the early Buddhist schools over the nature of truth and reality. That doctrine was sparked into a flame by the winds of controversy, whose currents can be seen in the material preserved in this text's description of the Vaibhāṣika views on the two truths.[1]

The doctrine of the two truths gave shape to questions throughout the entire range of scholastic Buddhist speculation on perception and knowledge. Questions about what ultimately existed, how it could be perceived, and how it could be expressed, and how the Buddha had done so in the scriptures, were all interconnected. The doctrine of two truths, therefore, was concerned with the interpretation of language, the fitting expression of the doctrine, and with the proper interpretation of the world itself—what exists, how it exists, and how it can be truly known.

Ngawang Belden's exposition of his material follows the Gelukpa tradition of the Gomang College of Drepung Monastery, and so follows the earlier teacher and writer Jamyang Shayba ('Jam-dbyangs-bzhad-pa Ngag-dbang-brtson-'grus, 1648-1721). Ngawang Belden's book conveniently collects together a wealth of material from the scriptures and commentaries. The publication of this particular section of his book is justified by the fact that it depicts the Buddhist debate out of which the doctrine of two truths, through the critique of the Perfection of Wisdom, emerged into the foreground of Buddhist philosophy. It therefore opens a window (although refracted through centuries of commentarial layers) onto the historical beginnings of this doctrine. This piece of Ngawang Belden (and, indirectly, Jamyang Shayba) also supplements the ongoing publication of other portions of their work.[2]

Ancient Indian Speculation on Language and Reality

The Beginnings of Grammar

By the time of the Buddha (about 500 B.C.E.), the Indo-Aryan languages spoken on the Indian subcontinent had diverged so far from the earlier language of the Vedas that these sacred scriptures had become obscure, and interpretive commentaries had begun to appear. These commentaries were avowed attempts to clarify what had always been present in the Vedas, but had become hidden behind corrupt forms of speech, faulty oral transmission, and imperfect interpretation.

They were not meant to create something novel, but merely to preserve the original message of the texts and to insure that their transmission would continue without interference. What may seem now like original lines of thought in the commentaries were considered to have occurred solely through remembering (*smṛti*) what had once been revealed in full but had been forgotten until the commentaries had made them explicit. Although the commentaries were "remembered," the basic texts of the Vedas were "heard" (*śruti*), implying that they were transmitted and received intimately, from teacher's mouth to student's ear, and so without interruption or change from generation to generation.

Nevertheless, problems arose from the disparity between the outward words of the ancient texts and the meanings attributed to them. The problem involved in textual interpretation was conceived conservatively, as purifying the Vedic language and expunging encroachments on the texts. This meant standardizing correct forms and excising deviant ones, which included those of non-Vedic dialects. Changes and novel interpretations, as well as unusual vocabulary, grammatical structures, or pronunciations, had to be avoided, for it was impossible to improve what had originally been perfect. The concern to uncover and preserve the words of the texts for their ritual recitation stimulated the development of the science of grammar, culminating in the work of Pāṇini in about the fifth century B.C.E.

The Buddhists' attitude toward Pāṇini was ambivalent, as was their attitude toward Sanskrit. Although he was not a Buddhist, his work was so important that some later Buddhists attempted to include him and his work, somehow, in their fold. In the *Laṅkāvatāra Sūtra*, dated by modern scholars, based on historical and linguistic evidence, to the third-fourth centuries C.E., the Buddha is made to prophesy that, "the author of [the treatises on] grammar will be Pāṇini," and the fifth century C.E. *Mañjuśrī Mūlatantra* claimed that Pāṇini attained a moderate level of Buddhist enlightenment—that of the "hearer" (*śrāvaka*) level.

The Tibetan Buddhist historian Bu-dön (Bu-ston, 1290-1364) wrote that Pāṇini propitiated the deity Mahādeva in order to receive divine teachings on grammar. Mahādeva then uttered the sounds *a*, *i*, and *u*, and "by this Pāṇini came to apprehend the whole of the grammatical science."[3] Nevertheless, a version of the story in the *Mañjuśrī Mūlatantra* had explained that Pāṇini had propitiated the Buddhists' own Avalokiteśvara instead of Mahādeva.

Grammarians elaborated their science to defend the language of the Vedas from a loss of meaning, but they also understood it to be their duty to keep the mother language itself pure. The yogic philosopher and grammarian Patañjali (second century B.C.E.) stated that the preservation of the Vedas in their exact form was the most important reason for studying grammar. As an example, however, he said that the explicit statement of a correct form, like *gauḥ* ("cow"), also has the effect of implicitly negating corrupt forms, like *gāvī*, *gonī*, and *gotā*, which happened to be dialect-based variations of the word.[4] Patañjali here expressed the traditional idea that the various Indic dialects were degenerate forms of a single, primordial, pure Sanskrit. Modern scholars, however, believe that the Aryans brought more than one dialect of Indo-Aryan with them into India, and point out that the language of the Vedas is itself not uniform but variable.[5]

The efficacy of the ritual sacrifice depended on the priest's absolutely correct recitation of the Vedic formulas and invocations. Some linguistic historians derive the primitive impetus for the development of grammar from this necessity, which was effected by a pronunciation technique called *pada-patha*, whereby each word was repeated separately, but "to do this correctly . . . involved the beginning of grammatical analysis, and, since it involved the resolution of sandhi, phonetic analysis."[6]

Sandhi is the combination or transformation of sounds at the beginning and end of words when they are joined to other words, characteristic of Sanskrit and other Indo-Aryan languages that are akin to it. The transformations can sometimes obscure the words, as they would occur by themselves, causing some confusion about their meaning. An often told, apocryphal story—not originally Buddhist but taken up and repeated by Buddhist historians Tāranātha (b. 1575) and Bu-dön—described the problem of sandhi when they told the story of how the study of grammar was supposed to have begun. One day a king, playing with his wives in a pond, said to one of them, "*Mā udakam dehi*"—"Don't splash water on me." Being from a different region, however, she understood him to have said, "*Modakam dehi*"—"Bring me sweets." She left the pond and returned shortly with sweets for her husband, but he became angry at the misunderstanding, and decided he would apply himself to studying how words should combine properly.[7]

Philosophical and Religious Issues Connected to Grammar

When students entered religious training as priests in the Vedic tradition, they began with the study of grammar, a practice that was continued in the Buddhist scholastic centers of ancient India.[8] They learned that grammar proceeded by analysis, breaking apart the verbal roots and stems from the prefixes, suffixes, conjugational and declensional endings, and from the sandhi, separating them from the networks of case relationships that formed the contexts in which they occurred.

The grammarian Bhartṛhari (fifth century C.E.) explained that grammarians "know the connection of words" and that interpretation was the "science of dividing words into elements and bringing out their exact meaning." He called this systematic grammatical analysis *smṛti* (the "remembered"), as opposed to the *śruti* (the "heard"), by which he meant the source texts upon which the grammatical analysis was done. His very use of these terms indicated that he believed that the legitimate interpretation of, or commentary on, a text, should, strictly speaking, stray no farther from it than a grammatical analysis will allow.[9] This conservatism in textual interpretation is consonant with Patañjali's statement in his *Mahābhāṣya* that a commentary should not add anything that is not already in the text, a directive which, if followed literally, would invalidate any comment whatsoever on the text.[10]

With such a rigid restriction on commenting on a text, interpreters resorted to uncovering the etymologies of words in the text. The etymology of a word pointed to its origin and therefore was believed to reveal its real meaning divested of secondary meanings and connotations accumulated through time and circumstance. The commentators believed that the etymology of a word was a sure guide to its real meaning, so the "discovery" of a surprising or "hidden" etymology for a term in a philosophical dispute decisively secured one's doctrinal position when it could be linked to the etymology. The pursuit of etymologies (*nirukta*) intensified to keep pace with the linguistic drift that had occurred between earlier and later forms. The temptation to uncover hidden but (in truth) mistaken etymologies for word forms simply based on tortured similarity of sounds must have been great. Modern linguists have pointed to numerous instances when the ancient commentators asserted that words had certain etymologies, based more on their imagination than on the actual derivations of the words.[11] If the obscurity of the language of the received texts made the development of a science of etymology necessary, it also encouraged its excessive application.

Underlying the excessiveness was the notion that all words could be analyzed into "substantives" (*dravya*) or into "nouns" or "names" (*nāman*). These names were supposed to be the true names of the constituents of the world, and they were ultimately built from grammatical roots. By distinguishing these names, one could discern the true names of real things. One might even conjure them, for the pronunciation of these names was often said to have an immense ritual and magical power. Nevertheless, even in the earliest example of a sustained work on etymology, Yāska's *Nirukta*, which he wrote about the turn of the sixth century B.C.E., a debate on this subject is described between two grammarians, Śākaṭāyana and Gārgya. Śākaṭāyana held that all nouns could be derived through etymological and grammatical analysis from verbal roots, and Gārgya held that all of them could not. Later Sanskrit grammarians reflected Śākaṭāyana's position, for the most part. It is also evident in the willingness of the Nyāya-Vaiśeṣika philosophical school to posit real substances (*dravya*) corresponding to every linguistically meaningful entity, even those not ordinarily regarded as substantives, such as words like "and" and "or," which they included in a category of phenomena they called "relations."[12]

The Grammarians, considered as a coherent philosophical school, and the Mīmāṃsā ("inquiry," "exegesis") School, whose aim was the conservative defense of the Vedas, held that a close, ineluctable connection existed between the precise form of a word and its meaning. The Mīmāṃsakas held, as one of their main doctrines, that, "Sound is permanent." In this, they expressed their belief that the words of the Vedas were eternal and immortal and were not created by human agency. In Indian society, where writing was still a novelty, words were regarded as essentially sounds.

This "sound" (*śabda*) was the sound of the Vedas, permanent because the Vedas were eternally true. Patañjali invoked this idea at the beginning of his *Mahābhāṣya* by declaring that "the relationship (*sambandha*) between a word (*śabda*) and its meaning (*artha*) is fixed (*siddha*)."[13] He then carefully glossed *siddha* ("fixed," "established") as synonymous with *nitya* ("permanent," "eternal"), and as the opposite of *kārya* ("produced"). He used *siddha* in this case, he said, with the same meaning that it had in the expressions "the eternal sky" (*siddhā dyauḥ*), "the eternal earth" (*siddhā pṛthivī*), and "eternal space" (*siddham ākāśam*), as opposed to the meaning it had in the expressions "the rice is ready" (*odanaḥ siddhaḥ*) and "the pea soup is done" (*sūpaḥ siddhā yāvāgur iti*), which referred to products (*kārya*).

Patañjali and other later grammarians and the Mīmāṃsakas, even when asserting that sounds or words were permanent, attempted to avoid claiming, as a result, that when people utter words, either the sound they make has no beginning or end, or that they do not actually produce or create it. Patañjali distinguished two meanings of *śabda*—the first was, for example, the impermanent vocal tone (*dhvani*) that is the sound people make when they speak, and the second was the eternal and intermittently manifesting word that is the conveyor (*sphoṭa*) of meaning.[14] The relationship between these two was, however, admittedly difficult to describe, and other schools rejected the distinction as incoherent. The Naiyāyikas and the Buddhists, in particular, emphatically declared that *śabda* ("sound") is *anitya* ("impermanent"). For the Buddhists anyway, this was consistent with their effort to distance themselves from the authority of the Vedas.[15]

The Mīmāṃsā School embarked on the work of standardizing Sanskrit, just as the Grammarians did. The Mīmāṃsakas, however, always gave precedence to Vedic Sanskrit and were wary of the precedence gradually achieved by the form of Sanskrit described by Pāṇini, which we now refer to as "classical Sanskrit." To the Mīmāṃsakas, Vedic was the originally pure language, in which the god Brahmā spoke and through which he created the universe. Another mythological explanation identified the goddess Vāc as the speaker. She was later identified with the goddess Sarasvatī, the consort of Brahmā. She emitted sounds, and in doing so created the realm of discourse. Moreover, her emission of sounds actually created the world. This led to the notion that the universe was essentially a network of syllables or letters, each of which was a seed (*bīja*) with a specific power (*śakti*) with which it could interact with others.

By concentrating on this network and its structure, revealed through grammatical analysis, or even by reciting the alphabet (*varṇapatha*) or another set of letters, one could mentally retrace the world's evolution back to its source, dissolving the elaborated complexes of speech into their primary units—that is, Brahmā's speech.[16] This suggests why studying language and grammar was so important. Bhartṛhari wrote that, "Vāc reveals herself to those who analyze speech."[17] Grammatical analysis was therefore an analysis of the structure of reality itself.

Bhartṛhari developed a theory that the world was produced by sound, and evolved (*vivarta*) or was elaborated through a process that mirrored grammatical transformations.[18] The single sound that Brahmā (or Vāc) was said to have spoken and which elaborated itself into the universe was *Aum*, the syllable uttered at the beginning and end of the recitation of the Vedas. Buddhists had already theorized a similar process consisting of the periodic evolution (*vivṛtta*) and dissolution or contraction (*saṃvṛtta*) of the universe. Nevertheless, they explicitly rejected Bhartṛhari's idea insofar as the Mīmāṃsakas and, later, the Vedāntins (who called it *śabdādvaita*, "non-duality of sounds") formulated it into a theory of transformation that explained the material world. The Buddhists said that the theory assumed the existence of a permanent essence that passed through merely superficial changes, contradicting the Buddhist principle of selflessness (*nairātmya*), according to which no real essence could maintain itself from moment to moment, even though subject to superficial "transformations" (*parināma*).

The Buddhists opposed the Mīmāṃsakas' notion of language, according to which words—that is, sounds—were essentially immutable, that they had a reality of their own apart from their use. In this respect, all Buddhists were nominalists. Not only did they assert that, "Sound is impermanent," but they argued against any inexorable or permanent connection between a particular word (or its form) and its meaning. The connection, they said, was merely conventional—established simply by agreement (tacit or not) among the word's users.

This eventually led the Buddhist philosopher Dharmakīrti (seventh century C.E.) to argue against the Mīmāṃsakas' belief that substantially existent universals imparted a measure of their substance to particulars, and led him to explain the phenomenon of linguistic reference in a different way. The meaning of a term does not come from some pre-existent positive correspondence between it and its referent, he said, but from a kind of exclusion principle in which a person learns first what the term excludes—what one might call its context—and then concludes what it refers to. The Buddhist philosopher Dignāga (fifth century C.E.) quoted Bhartṛhari's *Vākyapadīya* in his *Hetucakradamaru* in order to point out that the grammarian himself had admitted that, "People talk sentences, not words, and 'word' is an abstraction artificially analyzed out by grammarians."[19]

The Buddhists and the Hindu grammarians did not always advocate diametrically opposed positions. Some schools of Buddhism, for example, notably the Mahāsaṃghika and the schools of the Mahāyāna, developed a theory about the nature of the Buddha's speech (*Buddhavacana*) which in some respects resembled the non-Buddhist theory about the permanent "word of Brahmā." One difference between the two was that the non-Buddhists ultimately traced words and letters back to the eternal Brahmā, while the Buddhist philosophers of the Mahāyāna traced them back to emptiness (*śūnyatā*).[20] On the other hand, the Hindu grammarians sometimes admitted a kind of authority to the conventional meanings of words. Helārāja (late tenth century C.E.), for example, wrote that, "as a system of study entirely devoted to words and their popular signification, grammar does not care so much for strict adherence to reality or agreement of thought with truth, but takes words and their meanings as they are popularly used."[21] And, to complicate matters further, even philosophers who did not defend the Vedas and their language could use the eternalist view of language that the grammarians had originally expounded as a way to defend Sanskrit.

The Jains, for example, used a similar argument to demonstrate the preeminence of Ardhamāgadhī, the language of their own scriptures, and the language in which their founder, Mahāvīra, delivered his teachings. They considered all other languages—human and non-human—to have been derived from it: "The Lord propagated the law in the Ardhamāgadhī language; this Ardhamāgadhī, which gives peace, happiness, and bliss, undergoes modifications when it is spoken by the Āryans, the non-Āryans, the bipeds, the quadrupeds, the wild and the tamed animals, the birds, and the worms." And then, "We salute Vāc who is fully Ardhamāgadhī and who modifies herself into all the different languages, and who is perfect and omniscient."[22] Ardhamāgadhī is one of the many Indo-Aryan languages and dialects that are closely related to Sanskrit and that are together known by tradition—not Jain—as the Prakrits (*prākṛta*, "unrefined"), as opposed to Sanskrit (*saṃskṛta*, "refined").

Early Buddhist Views on Language, Truth, and Interpretation

Denying the Preeminence of Any Particular Language

The language the Buddha spoke was almost certainly one of the Prakrits, specifically a dialect of Māgadhī, and some evidence exists of a Buddhist scriptural canon in Māgadhī during the reign of the Buddhist King Aśoka (third century B.C.E.).[23] Nevertheless, the Buddha apparently advocated the phrasing of his teaching in whatever language was necessary in order to communicate with an audience:

> Now I know well that when I approached various large assemblies, even before I had sat down there or had spoken or begun to talk to them, whatever might have been their sort I made myself of like sort, whatever their language so was my language. And I rejoiced them with a talk on Dhamma [Skt. *dharma*], made it acceptable to them, set them on fire, gladdened them.[24]

The Chinese Buddhist canon contains a story in which the Buddha was said to have one day met the four "great celestial kings," to whom he preached a sermon. He spoke the first two verses of his text in Sanskrit, from which two of the kings became enlightened. The other two had not understood, and to communicate to them, he spoke the next verse in Tamil, which the third king understood, and then the next in a "barbarian" (*mleccha*) language, which the fourth king understood.[25]

The Buddha used whatever language it took to convey his meaning to his audience. This implied that the meaning was not utterly dependent on the particular form it took. That form was merely a convention, but the Buddha "conformed to the world" (*lokānuvartana*) by assuming its conventions. Another story, in the Chinese translation of the *Vinayamātṛkā*, emphasizes this point:

> Two monks who had been born as Brahmins approached the Buddha and said that since there were many sorts of people who were followers of the Buddha, from many different places, speaking many different languages, and that by putting the teachings in various dialects and languages, they distorted the Buddha's true meaning. These two monks wished to be allowed to revise and compile the sūtras of the Buddha according to the meter and linguistic form used in reciting the Vedic texts in order to make the meaning of the Buddha's scriptures clear. To their request, the Buddha replied: "In my doctrine, there is no justification for beautiful language. All that I desire is that the sense and the reasoning are not deficient. It is necessary to preach according to the pronunciation that allows beings to understand. That is why it is said to be suitable to conform oneself to the [various] lands."[26]

The style of scriptural recitation that he discounted was the one that Brahmins used to recite the Vedas, *pada-patha*, "in which each word (*pada*) is detached from the context and enunciated separately without undergoing any of the modification that grammatical euphony (*saṃdhi*) imposes in the interior of the phrase."[27] In this style, the words were separated one from the other in order to make all the parts explicit. The Brahmins believed that this was a purer style than a more "natural" one in which words were run together, where the environment of each sound could modify its pronunciation. This style was analogous to the grammatical analysis of discourse, in which each component was revealed in its true nature, free of the grammatical modifications imposed by context. It would also seem to have been at odds with the early Buddhist understanding of the way in which one grasped meaning through language, which may have been why the Buddha forbade this style of recitation.

Searching for the Final Doctrine

The Buddha and his followers made a distinction between conventional form and true meaning, between appearance and reality. In the *Dharmapada*, for example, the so-called "Brahmins" of the Buddha's time are said to lack those qualities that constitute what a true Brahmin should be. It was a new and incorrect idea, said the Buddha, that one became a Brahmin by birth, rather than by spiritual attainment. As a religious reformer, the Buddha rejected the worldly interpretation of a traditional term—"Brahmin"—that he said should refer to a deep spiritual reality. The person fit to be called a "Brahmin" was not necessarily the one that was conventionally or commonly designated as one. He did not call someone a "Brahmin," he said, because he had the ascetic's matted hair, or because he was born in a family of the Brahmin caste, but only because he was "free from impediments, free from clinging."[28] In the Vedic period, the word *brāhmaṇa* meant "sacred text," and so a Brahmin was one who possessed the sacred texts and their truth. But who really possessed that truth?

The Buddha rejected not only the Vedic texts themselves, but also other conventional forms of religion associated with the Vedic tradition, including the automatic birthright to spirituality given to the Brahmin caste. He sought the reality behind the conventional forms, the truth behind conflicting claims. In the *Sutta Nipāta*, he pointed out that the wandering ascetics and teachers of his day were nonsensically contentious and narrow-minded to the very extent that they thought that their own individual dogmas fully expressed the ultimate truth:

> What some say is the ultimate doctrine (*dhammam paramam*)
> Is just what others say is "low."
> What of these states the truth?
> For they all seem to be knowledgeable.
>
> Each one says his own doctrine is perfect
> And further, that the others' doctrine is "low,"
> And so they enter into dispute,
> Each one stating the conventional (*sammuti*) to be true.[29]

In one sense, therefore, the Buddha was a reformer and interpreter who appropriated concepts and terms from his culture and found new—or renewed—meaning there.[30] From this point of view, his doctrine only recovered what had been temporarily lost. In this sense, the Buddha devalued the established authority of the Vedas and encouraged the constant analysis and renewal of doctrine in order to reclaim the truth. He insisted that his monks test everything he said, analyzing it as a goldsmith cuts into a gold sample and melts and applies chemicals to it in order to test its purity. He said that they ought not to accept anything simply because he had said it.

In the *Kālama-sutta*, a group from the Kālama clan comes to him for guidance on how to regard the conflicting claims of the many wandering religious teachers of the time. He tells them, "Do not be led by report or by tradition or by hearsay. Be not led by the authority of religious texts . . . nor on the basis of the reliability of the person, nor out of respect for your teacher." They should instead use their own experience and reasoning, to determine for themselves whether something is good or bad.[31]

In the *Canki-sutta*, a young Brahmin asks the Buddha about the claim made for the Vedas that "this alone is true and all else is falsehood," which was based on the view that the Vedas gained their authority by tradition. In reply, the Buddha asks him if any of the Brahmins who have transmitted the Vedas can say, "I know this, I see this; this alone is true, all else is falsehood," to which the youth replies that none of them, even going back seven generations, can claim such direct knowledge. The Buddha then compares their tradition to a chain of blind men, each one holding onto the one ahead, making the point that a text's being revered by tradition is not sufficient grounds for accepting it as true.[32]

The early Buddhist search for truth consisted in analyzing or cutting through the surface complexity, the conventionalities, the extraneous elaborations, in order to find the underlying meaning or reality. The elaboration was sometimes a necessary sugar coating, as it were, for the powerful medicine the Buddha dispensed to disciples afflicted with various spiritual diseases. Those who were strong and intelligent, however, had no need for embroidered or oblique language. They could be given the essence of the teaching directly.

Such a disciple was Śāriputra, whose contemporaries considered him to be the Buddha's cleverest follower and most brilliant summarizer and expositor of the doctrine in the fashion of what was later known as the *abhidharma*—the "higher doctrine."[33] His ability to grasp the essence of the teaching was evident even on the occasion of his conversion to Buddhism, when he was able to achieve enlightenment merely by a monk's almost casual recitation of a brief summary of the meaning (*artha*) of the Buddha's teaching, that is, "Of all things that have arisen from causes, the Tathāgata has proclaimed the origin and also the cessation."[34]

Discerning the essential meaning of the doctrine, therefore, was much more important than knowing all its many forms. Several passages in the Pali scriptures maintain that although one can acquire knowledge of a text by memorizing it, even before one understands its meaning, the vigor and future well-being of the doctrine depends entirely on the disciples' understanding of its meaning.[35] They say that the parrot-like recitation of the doctrine, while perhaps creating some merit from the mere transmission of the doctrine, can as easily result in the doctrine's confusion and loss due to memory defects that are not corrected by knowledge of the doctrine's meaning. The best disciples, it is said, know both the meaning and the proper form of the doctrine.

Collecting and Standardizing the Teaching

The Buddha intended that his disciples avoid sectarianism and blind adherence to tradition in matters of doctrine and scripture, but he did standardize a group of rules embodying the monks' behavioral discipline (*vinaya*).[36] The monks recited these rules at certain times of year when they gathered into a community. The recitation accompanied a confessional ceremony during which the monks declared their infractions before the entire assembly. The monks also generally memorized and recited at least a small collection of the Buddha's teachings that were set to verse. This set of teachings was, in the early texts, simply referred to as the *dharma* ("doctrine").[37] It was later expanded and prose sections were included and it became known as *sūtra* (Pali *sutta*, literally, "thread," but used to mean "precept" in the Vedic literature and "discourse" of the Buddha in this Buddhist usage).

One reason the Buddha would have standardized his teachings despite repeatedly warning his disciples against blind adherence to scriptures is given in a story that is repeated twice in the Pali canon. Here, the Buddha's disciple Ānanda tells the Buddha about quarreling and violence that have arisen among the followers of the ascetic teacher Nāṭaputta, who had recently died. His disciples were arguing over the exact phrasing of his doctrine, accusing one another of having confused the order of certain words. Their quarreling had scandalized the lay disciples of the dead teacher and had destroyed the ascetic discipline of those who were his monks. Ānanda was apparently worried that something similar might happen after the Buddha passed away.

The Buddha responded by describing a way in which his monks were to assemble and, without quarreling, "rehearse" the doctrine, "comparing meaning with meaning, and phrase with phrase," in order to maintain it. He then gave a summary list of his most important teachings, which he called "truths." These included the four foundations of mindfulness (Pali *satipaṭṭhāna*, Skt. *smṛtyupasthāna*), the four right exertions (Pali *sammappadhāna*, Skt. *samyakpradhāna*), the four magical powers (Pali *iddhipāda*, Skt. *ṛddhipāda*), the five spiritual faculties (Pali, Skt. *indriya*), the five powers (Pali, Skt. *bala*), the seven limbs of enlightenment (Pali *bojjaṅga*, Skt. *bodhyaṅga*), and the noble eightfold path (Pali *maggaṭṭhaṅga*, Skt. *mārgāṣṭāṅga*).

In one version of the story, the Buddha says that he is not as concerned about the monks' differences of opinion about the particulars of their behavioral discipline or *vinaya*, as he is concerned about their differences of opinion about the nature of the path to enlightenment and how to cultivate that enlightenment, topics which are described in the summary of doctrine, or *sūtra*.[38] The way in which this *sūtra* form would preserve his teaching is explained in the *vinaya* of the Dharmaguptaka sect. There, the Buddha speaks of the fate of the teachings of previous Buddhas, who had appeared in the world many eons before:

> Even when those Buddhas and the assembly of the disciples died, the people of this world, of different names, families, and clans, and those who had left the householder's life, did not allow the doctrines to be soon extinguished. Why? Because they had drawn them up together in the form of *sūtra*

> ["thread"]. Śāriputra, it is as if, for example, various flowers strung upon a thread were put on a table, and although the wind might blow, they would not be scattered. Why? They were stitched and drawn together with the thread.[39]

These and other sources provide evidence that a Buddhist canon was to be determined by mutual agreement (Pali *sammatā*) on texts that were remembered and then recited in the presence of the community.[40] Hammering out the standard version of the texts was said to have begun at the first Buddhist council, at Rājagṛha, immediately after the Buddha's final nirvāṇa. At that council, Ānanda was said to have recited the *sūtra* collection and another monk was said to have recited the *vinaya.*

Various Buddhist schools preserved different accounts of the earliest councils, but most emphasized that all the monks who were present helped to determine the correct form of the texts through their constructive criticism as people recited them. The Mahāsaṃghika's version, for example, says that the monk who had been voted to recite the *vinaya* rules before the assembly told his fellow monks before he began that they should interrupt and correct him if his memory strayed.[41] Even the Mahīśāsaka School's version, in which one monk acts as a final judge of orthodoxy, still gives all the monks "a deliberating as well as a consulting voice in the debate." Buddhists may not have had a formal ecclesiastical board of appeal in matters of doctrine—apart from the entire monastic community itself. Nevertheless, the history of the early schools demonstrates that different groups standardized the doctrine in various ways, and that these differences formed the basis of sectarian disputes about the Buddha's true teaching.

The Growth of the Abhidharma

The Buddha's insistence that his disciples constantly analyze and seek the truth behind what simply presented itself to them as the truth was reflected in the four reliances (Pali *patisaraṇa,* Skt. *pratisaraṇa*):

1. Rely on the doctrine (*dharma*) and not on the man (*puruṣa*) [that is, the teacher].

2. Rely on the meaning (*artha*) and not on its elaboration (*vyañjana*).
3. Rely on sūtras of literal meaning (*nītārtha*) and not on sūtras the meaning of which must be drawn out (*neyārtha*) [that is, interpreted or inferred].
4. Rely on direct knowledge (*jñāna*) and not on discursive knowledge (*vijñāna*).[42]

The contrasts within these four "reliances" suggest that within the diversity of appearances, which offer contradiction and inconsistency, it is both possible and necessary for the Buddha's disciples to extract the pure kernel of truth. This was the goal of interpretation. The Buddha himself had done it, as described in the story about Ānanda's anxiety over the fate of the teaching, when he enumerated lists of his true doctrine, his basic teachings. The contents of his first sermon, preached at the Deer Park near Varanasi, also epitomized all his teachings. In this sermon, he preached the four noble truths, which outlined the ills of the world as well as the way of deliverance. These four truths were those of suffering, its origin, its cessation, and the path leading to its cessation. Some schools came to consider these four "truths" as categories into which components of the objective world could be put—that is, "true sufferings," "true origins," "true cessations," and "true paths."[43]

The systematic abstraction of the most essential doctrines, which the Buddha himself began, was extended to the *sūtra* collection as a whole. This began with appending resumes or tables of contents to the beginning of the various sūtras. These served as memory aids for those who were memorizing them, as well as teaching outlines. In Pali they were called *mātikā* (Skt. *mātṛkā*, literally, "mother-text," "root-text," "model"). These grew longer and more elaborate as time passed. They were eventually collected together apart from the sūtras they had meant to summarize and became a collection in their own right, independent of the sūtras. As the *mātṛkā* assumed this independence, their concise lists of terms and definitions were more formally organized around particular subjects, the information on which was culled from many sources rather than from single sūtras. At the same time, the compilers tended to fill in the "gaps" in the lists with things or terms that they understood the Buddha to have implicitly taught in the sūtras.

The collection of *mātṛkā* eventually came to be called the *abhidharma*—that is, the "higher doctrine," distinguishing it from the (mere) *dharma*, that is to say, the *sūtra*.[44] Most Buddhist schools came to give the *abhidharma* at least equal rank with the *vinaya* and *sūtra*, and divided the Buddhist canon into three sections as a result. Some Buddhist writers actually gave the *abhidharma* precedence over the other two because they regarded it as the essence of the doctrine contained in the *sūtra*—how could such a purified form of the doctrine not take precedence over the doctrine in its unorganized form?[45] The *abhidharma*, in this way, became the standard and the touchstone for doctrinal truth—it was the key for unlocking the Buddha's discourses.

Because an independent *abhidharma* was considered by some of its enthusiasts—such as the Sarvāstivādins—to have been simply abstracted from the Buddha's teachings in the *sūtra*, they did not question its authenticity as the word of the Buddha (*Buddha-vacana*). But some other Buddhists—the Sautrāntika School, for example—strongly opposed the claim that such an independent *abhidharma* was actually the "word of the Buddha." It would seem that they wished to retain the precedence of the sūtras. They admitted that the Buddha did indeed have an *abhidharma*, in the sense of a higher or final doctrine, but they said that this was diffused throughout the sūtras themselves and could not be separated from them, as the Sarvāstivādins had done with their seven *abhidharma* treatises, and still be truly regarded as the "word of Buddha."[46] The Sautrāntikas also believed that the Sarvāstivādins had fabricated some of the categories in their systematization of the Buddha's teachings.

In the *Aṭṭhasālinī*, Buddhaghosa addressed Buddhist critics who denied that the *abhidharma* section of the canon was actually preached by the Buddha.[47] One reason the critics gave for denying the canonical status of the *abhidharma* was that, unlike the *sūtra* and the *vinaya*, the *abhidharma* books did not have frame stories that gave the details of when and where the Buddha had preached them. Buddhaghosa gave two reasons why one should believe that the Buddha preached them: first, the doctrines found there were so profound that only a Buddha could have taught them, and second—borrowing an argument from the Mahāyāna—the Buddha first preached the *abhidharma* in other worlds (that is, in the heavens), and that is the reason that no ordinary settings of time and place are given in the *abhidharma* texts.

Pārśva, one of the authors of the Sarvāstivāda School's *Mahāvibhāṣā*, replied to a criticism made by the Sautrāntikas (whose name means "those who rely on *sūtra* as final"). They said that certain *abhidharma* doctrines had no justification in the sūtras.[48] To meet this criticism, Pārśva made the extraordinary claim that the reason these matters could not be found in the sūtras must be because they had been in sūtras that the Buddha had preached, but that had been subsequently lost. The principle—or perhaps anti-principle—is achieved by a reversal. At first the word of the Buddha was used as the standard by which to judge various statements. Later a standard, in the form of a true principle, was set by which to judge whether something was the word of the Buddha. Scholars have contrasted the statement carved into the Bhabra Rock Edict—"Whatever is spoken by the Buddha is well spoken"—with a passage from the Mahāyāna *Adhyayasamchodana Sūtra* which Prajñākaramati quotes, where the Buddha says, "Anything . . . that is well said is the word of the Buddha."[49]

The inference of the past existence of what were in fact historically dubious teachings, based on general principles, was analogous to the Sanskrit grammarians' back-formation of hundreds of Sanskrit roots that no one ever found in actual use but which they assumed existed by using the principles of grammatical formation at work in the (later) language which they had discerned and generalized.[50] A similar kind of process, involving back-formation, was invoked, typically, by Mahāyāna writers to explain where their Perfection of Wisdom and Mahāyāna sūtras (and later their tantras) came from—they had to agree that these texts had not been in the scriptural collections. But rather than agreeing with the non-Mahāyāna Buddhists that people were writing them anew—that is, were forging them and trying to pass them off as authentic—they shared the notion among them that the Buddha had in fact taught these, but not to human audiences—rather, he had taught them to other beings in other realms or worlds because they were prepared to understand and accept them, or because they would safeguard them, hidden away from human awareness until the time that humans had progressed enough to appreciate them.[51]

The gist of the argument, however, was not unique to the Mahāyāna schools, but must have been present quite early in the tradition because even the conservative Theravādins' version of the *Aṅguttara-nikāya* argues that, in the same way that one could infer that people carrying baskets of grain had gotten it from a granary, so one could infer that something that is well said is the word of the Buddha.[52] The Theravādin commentator Buddhaghosa even included, in the word of the Buddha, the *Kathāvatthu,* a collection of doctrinal debates between the Theravādins and representatives of other Buddhist schools. Moggaliputta Tissa compiled it around the time of the third Buddhist council (around 250 B.C.E.). Buddhaghosa admitted that the book had its historical basis at that time, but argued that the Buddha had known and approved of its contents during his lifetime, anticipating the debates through his ability to see more than two hundred years into the future.[53]

The Buddha's Word

The Truth behind the Multitude of Forms

Early Buddhist views on the how the Buddha had expressed himself in the conventions of language were diverse. Some schools, such as the Mahāsaṃghika, held that all languages were equally capable of conveying the Buddha's teachings. Some schools, however, such as the Sarvāstivāda, distinguished one language or one set of terms as primary and all others as derivative and more or less deviant, and therefore less capable of conveying the Buddha's ultimate truth. The range of opinion on this point also affected the various schools' attitude toward writing down the scriptures, that is, using the conventions of writing to present the teachings.[54]

Even in Vedic times, manuscripts were used as auxiliaries in the oral instruction on the Vedas, in the same way that, later, the Buddhists' *mātṛkā* texts were developed as teachers' outlines or memory aids. The Buddhist texts were transmitted orally at first, which was consonant with the Vedic notion that it was the oral transmission of a sacred text that carried its essence and kept it alive.

When the Buddhists committed all their texts to writing, however, they did so with a variety of motives. The linguistically conservative Theravādins, for example, acted in order to prevent deviation from the original teaching and to use writing as a means to stabilize or fix the tradition.[55] During the period when they wrote down the scriptures, 35-32 B.C.E., wars and plague threatened the Sinhalese kingdom in which they lived. The monks were fearful that texts would disappear altogether if the ranks of monks—who memorized the texts—became depleted. With a Buddhist appreciation for the impermanence of things, they realized that the Buddha's teachings might disappear from the world, and so, to prevent that, they recorded their texts in writing. This was an effort to counter what they believed was the natural process of deterioration of the Buddhist teaching in the world, perhaps until the time that another Buddha could establish his teaching. Writing down the scriptures was a revolutionary step for the time—the Buddhists were the first in the Indian cultural region to do so. Until then, writing was thought of as simply a tool of commerce and politics, not something capable of conveying the power of a sacred text.[56]

This may seem like a kind of liberalizing idea—putting the scriptures into written form. The conservative Theravādins, however, were primarily motivated by the conviction that the scriptures of their own specific community, as distinct from the scriptures held by other Buddhist schools, were the only uncorrupted collection of the Buddha's words. If the Pali canon disappeared, therefore, so did the Buddha's teaching because Pali was the basic language of his doctrine and the one in which he expressed the truth directly, without having to adapt or compromise it for less than ideal audiences. Writing, therefore, was a tool, adopted in extreme circumstances, which allowed the standardization and conservative protection of orthodoxy.

Other Buddhist schools, however, like the Dharmaguptakas, carried the Buddha's doctrine to the far reaches of Asia, under the assumption that the Buddha's truth could be fully expressed in any language, and to all people.[57] They believed that the teaching was not tied to a particular form or culture or language, but was universal. For them, writing down the scriptures was a way to multiply and disseminate copies of them, rather than a way merely to preserve them. This idea—more liberal and universalistic—was typical of the Mahāyāna. The earliest printed texts of any sort that still exist are copies of the sūtras of the Perfection of Wisdom—the block-printing technology that was used to print them, and thousands of other copies, would seem to have been perfectly suited for the mass accumulation of merit that the printers would acquire for copying and disseminating them. It was the written form of the scriptures that attended the diffusion of the Buddhist doctrine throughout India and its singular success outside of India as well. Those who produced these scriptures believed it was possible to translate them into various dialects and languages and still convey the truth to all people, conforming and adapting the teaching to them.

The role of Sanskrit in Buddhism was unique because of its pride of place among the followers of the Vedas, who had, in an important sense, constructed it as a sacred language. At first, the Buddhists collected their scriptures in one or more Prakrit versions.[58] And they refrained from producing a Sanskrit version because of the language's connection with the Vedic tradition and philosophy. In time, some schools compiled the Buddhist scriptures in the artificial forms now known as "Buddhist hybrid Sanskrit" or "mixed Sanskrit," which were intermediate forms between the Prakrits and Sanskrit.

Eventually, the Sarvāstivāda School and its later offshoot, the Mūlasarvāstivāda, put the scriptures and treatises into classical Sanskrit, and it was Sanskrit that ultimately served as the *lingua franca* for the development of scholastic Buddhism in India. Despite its later, nearly universal use in Indian Buddhism, however, the various schools regarded it differently. Some schools, such as the Mahāsaṃghika, treated it as merely one convenient form that happened to be understood by many people, but that was merely one among many possible languages in which the truth could be conveyed. Others, however—such as the Sarvāstivāda—accorded it the unique honor that was given it in non-Buddhist circles. It alone, they believed, perfectly conveyed the truth. Other languages opened the door to confusion and misunderstanding

The Sarvāstivādins passed along a story in which the Buddha's close disciple Ānanda—who had recited the *sūtra* collection at the first council—had grown old.[59] One day he happened to overhear a young monk reciting a verse from the *Dharmapada*. In the way he recited it, the meaning might be rendered this way:

> If a man were to live for a hundred years and not see
>   a water-heron,
> It were better that he live only for one day and see
>   a water-heron.

Hearing this, Ānanda told the young monk that the Buddha had not said that. Rather, what he had said was:

> If a man were to live for a hundred years and not see
> the principle of coming into existence and passing away,
> It were better that he live only for one day and see the
> principle of coming into existence and passing away.

The young monk told this to his own teacher, who offered the opinion that Ānanda was an old fool, and that the monk should continue his recitation according to the way he had originally received it. When Ānanda heard him continue with his faulty recitation, he realized that he could not correct the text just by himself, nor could he appeal to his own elders in the monastic community as authoritative since all the others from the early days had passed away. Realizing this, says the story, Ānanda decided not to delay his passing away any longer.

This story turns on Ānanda's having heard the young monk recite the verse in Prakrit. The Prakrit *udaka-vaya,* which means "coming into existence and passing away," corresponds to the Sanskrit (or Pali) *udaya-vyayam.* The Prakrit phrase, however, if taken as Sanskrit (or Pali) can mean "water-heron" (*udaka-vaya*). The Sarvāstivādins, with this story, would therefore seem to have been conveying more than just a general warning against the blind acceptance of texts without understanding their meaning, but also a more specific warning against one particular version, the Prakrit, implying that the Sanskrit version was the true one and the Prakrit a corrupt copy. In this light, the story is remarkably similar in sentiment to the story about the king who commanded his wife to stop splashing him with water, which assumed the preeminence of Sanskrit as the primordial, pure language.

The Sarvāstivādins' treatment of Sanskrit as the world's root-language is also evident in their interpretation of the story of the Buddha's preaching to the four kings in different languages.[60] On the face of it, it would seem that the point of the story was that the Buddha was free to use whatever language suited his listener. The Sarvāstivādins, however, said that it was significant that the Buddha had first used Sanskrit, and then afterwards had resorted to other languages. This meant, they thought, that he condescended to use these other languages only in order to communicate with the kings who did not understand Sanskrit, even though these other languages were second rate. This meant that Sanskrit was the Buddha's native language, which he modified on occasion, but purely out of necessity.

The Mahāsaṃghikas, however, believed that no language had any absolute priority over any other. The Buddha simply spoke to everyone according to the specific linguistic disposition of each. His truth was not tied to any particular language. They were all mere conventions.

The Sarvāstivādins asked the Mahāsaṃghikas what they believed the Buddha's native language was. The real nature of the Buddha's word, they answered, could not be specified or defined by the outlines of any single language. In fact, the Buddha's speech was ineffable. It was a "single sound" (*ekaśabda*), like an echo from an empty sky. It was not meaningful in itself, but carried an infinite potential, and was elaborated into any number of expressions or languages in order to conform to his listeners. Even though the Buddha may speak in one language, they said, "this utterance becomes current everywhere, even in the barbaric assemblies of the Scythians, the Greeks, the Chinese, the Ramathas, the Persians, and the Darodas."[61]

The Sarvāstivādins asked their opponents in this debate why then it was the case that the celestial kings who did not understand Sanskrit did not understand the Buddha immediately, when he spoke the first two verses of his sermon, even though the other kings heard them in Sanskrit, for if the Buddha had spoken a "single (ineffable) sound," which was simultaneously and instantaneously transformed into all other languages, all the kings should have understood him simultaneously.

The Mahāsaṃghikas replied that the latter two kings' own mental dispositions must have been faulty. They must have been incapable—as indeed were most people—of understanding the Buddha's teaching because of their internal, mental faults.

The Theravādins, like the Sarvāstivādins, took the conservative side of this issue of what we might regard as a debate as to whether one language corresponds to the true nature of the world in a way that others do not. Whereas the Sarvāstivādins said that Sanskrit was that language, however, the Theravādins said it was Pali—or, as they regarded it, Māgadhī—the language, they said, that the Buddha spoke.

The Theravādin Buddhaghosa wrote that Māgadhī (that is, Pali) was the "root language of all beings" and that its grammatically well-formed constituents were stable and contained no "deviant" (*vyabhicāra*) forms.[62] The proper etymologies and pronunciations of these components were invariable in that they had their "own being" (*sabhāva*). This was what allowed one to distinguish between correct, normative forms and incorrect, deviant ones. Buddhaghosa elaborated his linguistic theory in this way:

> A mother and father, laying their infant children down on a bed or a chair, talk to them while they do whatever they have to do. They determine what language the children will have by saying, "This is called this, this is called this." In the course of time, they come to know the entire language. If the mother is a Tamilī and the father is an Andhaka and if their baby hears the mother's speech first, then he will speak the Tamil language; if he hears the father's speech first, he will speak the Andha language. But if he does not hear the speech of either one, he will speak the Māgadhī language. Even if one is born in a great forest and never leaves it, a place where no names are ever pointed out, one will speak the Māgadhī language, that in which the speech of the doctrine arises.
>
> In the hells, among the animals, in the realm of the hungry ghosts, in the human world, and in the world of the gods, the Māgadhī language is present everywhere. The multitude of languages, such as the languages of Otta [Orissa], Kirāta, Andha, Yona [Greece], and Tamilā, are transformed out of it, but this one, which is called the "actual speech of Brahmā, the speech of Āryans," the Māgadhī language, has not been transformed at all.[63]

Buddhaghosa then tells his readers that the Buddha revealed the scriptural canon in "the same Māgadhī language that you use," and that the reason for this was that, since Māgadhī was constituted of the same sounds that vibrated everywhere, when the doctrine was spoken in Māgadhī to one who had "attained realization of the Buddha's speech," then merely a single sound needed to impinge on that person's ear and immediately the meaning was accompanied by a hundred or a thousand examples (*naya*) of it as well. Such a person was actually slowed down by wordy explanations. On the other hand, the same immediate realization of the word's ramifications was not possible working in other languages since they had to be constantly adjusted and brought into line—that is, with Māgadhī.

The Buddha's Ultimate Word and Ultimate Truth

The Mahāsaṃghikas' claim that the Buddha's words were reducible to a "single sound" would certainly have seemed to other schools as a doctrine unacceptably close to the Mīmāṃsakas' doctrine of the eternal "sound" of the Vedas that the god Brahmā spoke. This speech was antecedent to all particular forms of speech. It was a single sound as it was broadcast, but multiplied and transmuted itself to conform to the specific ears of various listeners. Making the Buddha's speech ethereal, universal, and ineffable was one part of the general revaluation of the nature of the Buddha and his teachings that occurred in Indian Buddhism and that later manifested itself in the Mahāyāna. According to this view, the particularities—one might say limitations—found in the Buddha's words, or in the events of his life as Śākyamuni, were not ultimately real. He was instead an unlimited, cosmic, wholly perfect and spiritual being whose life and various teachings were all parts of a multifaceted performance of appearances that he orchestrated in order to teach beings how to live and how to achieve nirvāṇa. It was a view that brought to the foreground the question of distinguishing between appearance and reality in the scriptures' descriptions of the Buddha's life and teachings. The distinction was between the Buddha's conventional nature and teaching—which he adopted "in conformity with the world"—and his ultimate nature and teaching.

Even those schools that did not align themselves with the Mahāyāna, however, also found plenty in the scriptures that they set about to explain in a way that would demonstrate that the Buddha was not limited in the same ways that ordinary beings were. In the Sarvāstivādins' *Mahāvibhāṣā*, various incidents in the Buddha's life were interpreted in a way that contradicted a literal reading of the canon. One had to look behind these incidents, according to the interpreters, to understand the Buddha's ulterior motives. Often, his real motive was to lead his disciples to do just the opposite of what he did. He was testing their independence and spiritual maturity. Or, these incidents were examples of his holding up a mirror to his disciples' imperfections. This was the case, for example, in his choice of words, in which some might have seen hatred. "He often treats his monks," one scholar explains, "as 'confused people' (*mohapurūṣa*); according to him, the young Brahmin Ambastha who lays claim to noble lineage is but the 'son of a slave of the Śākyas.'"[64] Not only that, the Buddha described Devadatta, his errant cousin who caused schisms in the monastic community and who tried to murder the Buddha and take control of the monks, as a "fool" (*mudha*), a "corpse" (*sava*), and a "lickspittle" (*kheṭasika*). But he intended no harm by these words, they said. It was only the corrective rebuke of a loving father to a wayward son.

Such an exegesis of these texts may be rather creative, but surely they are not as unrestrained as an exegesis that discounts all the distinctions made in the texts as "merely conventional"—that is, as ultimately false—and locates ultimate truth only outside the texts in an ineffable reality. If the particulars of the texts were simply chronicles of the Buddha's conforming himself to the obscure limitations of the world, rather than straightforward representations of his ultimate truth, then these particulars lost much of their power to set the standard for doctrinal truth. If the Mahāsaṃghikas (and their doctrinal heirs, the Mahāyāna) believed that all the scriptures were false or fictional—at least in some sense—then what could prevent them from producing new, bogus scriptures that they wrote in order to provide evidence for their own peculiar views? Or so their opponents apparently believed.

The first and most fundamental schism that occurred in the monastic community was between the Sthaviravādins (from which, among the schools considered here, evolved the Sarvāstivāda and the Theravāda) and the Mahāsaṃghika School, many of whose views were taken up into the Mahāyāna. The Theravādins accused the Mahāsaṃghika School of fraud and misrepresentation regarding the scriptures:

> The Bhikkhus of the Great Council [*Mahāsaṃghītikā*] settled a doctrine contrary (to the true Faith). Altering the original

> redaction, they made another redaction. They transposed Suttas that belonged to one place (in the collection), to another place; they destroyed the (true) meaning and the Faith [*dhamma*] in the Vinaya and the five collections (of Suttas). Those Bhikkhus, who understood neither what had been taught as not having to be followed to the letter [*pariyāya-desita*] nor what was taught as having to be followed to the letter [*nippariyāya-desita*], neither the literal meaning [*nītaṭṭham*] nor the meaning to be drawn out [*neyyaṭṭham*] attributed to that which was said with a certain intention [*sandhāya bhaṇita*] another sense (other than the true one); these Bhikkhus destroyed a great deal of (the true) meaning by their being obscured by the letter [*vyañjanacchāyāya*]. Rejecting single passages of the Suttas and of the profound Vinaya, they composed other Suttas and another Vinaya, which had only the appearance (of the genuine ones). Rejecting the following texts, viz.: the Parivāra, which is an abstract of the contents (of the Vinaya), the six sections of the Abhidhamma, the Paṭisambhidā, the Niddesa, and some portions of the Jātaka, they composed new ones. Forsaking the original rules regarding nouns, genders, composition, and the embellishments of style, they changed all that.[65]

The Sarvāstivādins maintained the conservative orientation of the Sthaviras in relation to the Mahāsaṃghikas. The Sarvāstivāda sectarian and historian Vasumitra (first century C.E.) contrasted the doctrines of the original Sarvāstivādins with those of the Mahāsaṃghikas.[66]

The Mahāsaṃghikas believed that all of the Buddha's discourses could be reduced to the noble eightfold path and the four noble truths, which he explained in his first sermon, at Sarnath, after his enlightenment. Not only that, but everything that he taught is in conformity with the truth, and is of direct meaning (*nītārtha*) because, ultimately, he expounded all his doctrines with a single utterance, not sequentially, nor even by arranging his words and sentences, or responding in order to questions. He pronounced that utterance all at once, from out of his non-discursive meditation, in a single act, and all his doctrines flowed out of it, instantaneously forming, of their own accord, the multitude of discourses that benefited his listeners.

The Sarvāstivādins, in contrast, believed that the Buddha, at Sarnath, taught only the noble eightfold path and the four noble truths—all his other teachings could not be reduced to these. They also held that the Buddha did not and could not expound all his doctrines with a single utterance, that he arranged his words and sentences in sequence, that some of the words he uttered did not conform to the truth (*ayathārtha*), and that some of his discourses were of direct or literal meaning (*nītārtha*) but some were not (*anītārtha*).

The various early schools' debates on conventional and ultimate truth were attempts to distinguish what really existed—the ultimate truth—from what the mind made of it, isolating patterns, multiplying entities, imagining thing, and therefore falsifying the truth. Distinguishing the two, in order to see the truth, without the ultimately false overlay of conceptual thought—what the world, by convention, regards as the truth—is the way to enlightenment. The "higher teaching," or *abhidharma*, distinguished the sūtras, one kind from another, based on the kinds of statements they contained, that is, based on the nature of the objects to which the statements referred. A "real teaching of the Buddha" was an ultimate truth, but an "imputation" (*prajñapti*) was a conventional truth.

In these early schools, however, a basic distinction remained in how they located the Buddha's ultimate truth. The Sarvāstivādins' method consisted in sifting the data presented in the scriptures in order to separate out the more important from the less important, to abstract the essence of the doctrine from the great mass of things he had taught. In the same way, they tried to distinguish those objects that the Buddha had said ultimately existed from those which did not, but which appeared to exist, based on the habits of convention. This method led them to formulate their *abhidharma*, which differentiated certain parts of the teaching, which they regarded as ultimately true, from others, which they regarded as only true conventionally.

The Mahāsaṃghikas and their heirs on this issue, however, sought simplicity and consistency in the ultimate truth by reducing all of the Buddha's teaching and all of the objects named in them to an ineffable underlying unity, which they regarded as the ultimate truth. The Mahāsaṃghikas said that all of the Buddha's teachings were derived from his ultimate teaching, and all of the particular objects named in his teachings rested on a deeper reality.

This approach is evident in the Perfection of Wisdom sūtras and in Nāgārjuna's treatises, where the basic teachings and most of the categories of the Sarvāstivādins' *abhidharma*—supposedly the ultimate truth—are examined and eventually wind up in the category of conventional truth.[67] The ultimate truth lies behind all this multiplicity and contradiction within the Buddha's teachings:

> Such are the multiple and diverse teachings; one who is ignorant and who hears them takes them for a perverse error, but the sage who penetrates the triple teaching of the doctrine knows that all the speeches of the Buddha are the true doctrine and do not contradict one another . . . Knowing that is the power of the Perfection of Wisdom, which, in the face of all the teachings of the Buddha, encounters no obstacle.[68]

A reading of the early Mahāyāna sūtras, including the Perfection of Wisdom sūtras, the *Laṅkāvatāra Sūtra*, and the *Avataṃsaka Sūtra*, strongly suggests that their authors were directing an attack on the Sarvāstivādins' *abhidharma* structure as superficial and an inadequate representation of the ultimate truth. Most of the categories of that structure, when they were accepted, were regarded as mere appearances, merely conventional, as opposed to the ultimate truth of emptiness.

This is by no means a full representation of Mahāyāna thought, however. In fact, the Mahāyāna did not discontinue the *abhidharma* categorization but intensified it. The Buddhist ideal of following the "middle way" made theorists wary of tending toward nihilism or "annihilation" if they were to give no measure of truth to conventional appearances but only regarded them as pure illusion. The *abhidharma* categories—now conventional truths—could not be negated by emptiness without damaging the Buddha's teachings. The commentarial literature is clear on this point, insisting that, as powerful as the doctrine of emptiness was, it did not overthrow the *abhidharma* categories; rather, it completed and perfected them, putting them in a true light. It showed them for what they were—conventional, not ultimate, truths.

The Perfection of Wisdom sūtras, therefore, did not negate the *abhidharma* structures; they were, instead, part of the *abhidharma* itself. Emptiness was made a category within it. In one way, emptiness pervaded all the categories of the *abhidharma*, indeed of all appearances whatsoever. In another way, emptiness, the ultimate truth, was merely one more category of the *abhidharma*, one more object in the real world, on a par with the other categories. Mahāyāna writers attempted to weave both strands of explanation into their presentations of the two truths, and tried to give a coherent interpretation that satisfactorily took into account both the most radical statements in the Perfection of Wisdom sūtras as well as the scholastic elaboration of the *abhidharma* theorists.

The Sarvāstivādins believed that less important details had been preserved in the sūtras along with the highest teachings.[69] This was the fundamental reason why they developed their *abhidharma*, for it was meant to contain the essence and ultimate meaning of the doctrines. The Mahāsaṃghikas took an opposing view. According to them, nothing that the Buddha said was essentially less important than anything else he said. He did everything for a reason; sometimes the reason was obvious, sometimes it was not. But if the meaning of his words and deeds was not immediately apparent, it was because of shortcomings in the disciple's or interpreter's understanding, not to any imperfection in the Buddha's statements or deeds themselves.

Very early in Buddhist doctrinal development, most schools came to regard the Buddha as having been omniscient (although the Theravādins' Pali canon preserves several texts that repudiate this claim). The Sarvāstivādins joined the general trend to regard the Buddha as omniscient, but they nevertheless held a "conservative" interpretation of what this meant, which can be contrasted with other interpretations, the Mahāsaṃghikas' for example.

According to the Sarvāstivādins, the Buddha could know anything he wished to know by merely directing his mind to it. Consequently, the questions he asked, such as when "he inquired about the weather and the rain from Ānanda and wanted to know where the loud cries in the monastery garden originated," could be regarded as merely rhetorical, because the Buddha could discover the answers himself merely by turning his mind to them.[70] Such questions had some deeper hidden purpose. His intention in asking them was actually to make some point, to teach something to those whom he questioned.

The Mahāsaṃghikas, in contrast, understood the Buddha's omniscience in a different way. They held that he simultaneously cognized everything in the universe. He did not gather information sequentially. His knowledge was completely non-discursive. He did not have to direct his mind anywhere because it was already there. They also held that the Buddha was always speaking, even though beings, because of their mental obscuration, might not always hear him, "just as thunder roars though the deaf are unable to hear it."[71] Even his silences were profoundly significant, for they did not indicate that he had nothing to say. Rather, everything the Buddha said and did was significant because he was always operating, one could say, at full power, whether or not one could immediately understand the import of his "ordinary" actions and words.

The further evolution of this understanding of the nature of the Buddha's teaching is illustrated by the differences in various interpretations of a passage from the *Dharmarātridvaya Sūtra.*[72] Buddhist exegetes from various schools denied that there were any real contradictions in the statements of the Buddha by citing this sūtra, which declared that everything that the Buddha spoke, from the night of his enlightenment to the night of his final nirvāṇa, was the truth and nothing else. An explanation was needed for apparent contradictions, however. In various sūtras, for example, the Buddha denied the existence of a "self" (*ātman*), but in other sūtras he spoke as if there existed a person or a Tathāgata—that is, the Buddha himself—or as if "beings" were seen with the Buddha's "divine eye."

The Mahāsaṃghikas' solution to the problem of seeming inconsistency was to claim that the contradictions lay not in the Buddha's expression of the truth but in the way in which his listeners received it. The Mahāsaṃghikas believed the Buddha spoke the simple truth in a single sound—the echo from empty space—and this belief passed to the Mahāyāna. In the *Lalitavistara*, a Mahāyāna revision of an originally Sarvāstivādin text which details the Buddha's miraculous life, he is said to "proclaim all speech by one speech." Paul Démieville explained the similar Mahāsaṃghika belief: "In virtue of his accumulated merits, the

Buddha has only to pronounce a single word, with a single emission of voice, in order to make the doctrine heard among beings, who interpret it differently according to their capacities and their needs." He paralleled this with a statement in the Mahāyāna *Avataṃsaka Sūtra*: "The Buddha makes use of a single sound to preach the doctrine to them, and does it in such a way that they gain intelligence, each according to his capacity. He causes those who are subject to desire, hatred, ignorance, or any of the eighty-four thousand different afflictions to hear those doctrines which serve as the antidotes to those afflictions." He also noted that the same doctrine is found in the Mahāyāna *Vimalakīrti Nirdeśa*, where the Buddha's "single sound" is said to be his "single doctrine." This was how he spoke "only the truth and nothing else." He broadcast all of it in a single emission of his voice.

The Mahāyāna *Avataṃsaka Sūtra* reduced all sounds whatsoever to the voice of the Buddha, and says that the Buddha's voice, since it is everywhere, is like an empty echo, produced from no definable source, yet manifested in various names that beings understand differently. His voice is said to extend itself without hindrance across the universe in every direction, conforming itself to each being who hears it. In reality, it has no specific origin in time or place, yet all sounds are manifested in it. He therefore enunciates nothing, yet all his doctrines are enunciated. The Mahāyāna *Laṅkāvatāra Sūtra* even says that the Buddha does not give discourses at all, and that "not speaking is the Buddha's speaking" (*avacanam Buddhavacanam*), a statement that quite clearly is meant to be understood from the *ultimate* point of view, not from the *conventional* one.

In this way, one no longer tries to sort out which teachings, words, or objects are ultimate from among a collection, assessing everything else as merely conventional. Instead, the ultimate is something beyond, or above, or below everything in the collection. All the individual items in that collection—of scriptures, words, or objects—are conventional truths that arise from out of that ultimate, like echoes from out of an empty sky. While in this view they lose their ultimately real individual significance and substance, they gain force as adaptable instrumentalities that point beyond themselves in various ways to the ultimate truth.

Definitive Sūtras and Those Whose Meaning Must Be Drawn Out

Most Buddhist schools maintained a division within the sūtras between those of direct meaning (*nītārtha*), that is, definitive sūtras, and those of indirect meaning (*neyārtha*), that is, sūtras whose meaning must be drawn out or inferred. But even among the schools that adhered to this distinction, no general agreement existed on what it meant.

The Sarvāstivāda (or Vaibhāṣika) historian Vasumitra reported that the early Sarvāstivādins claimed that among the discourses of the Buddha, some were definitive (*nītārtha*) and some were not definitive (*anītārtha*). This claim he contrasted with that of the Mahāsaṃghikas, who, he reported, claimed that all of the discourses of the Buddha were definitive (*nītārtha*). Perhaps this was meant to align with their view of the Buddha's "single utterance" that blossomed into the multitude of teachings, all of which could be traced back to him, no matter whether they were superficially inconsistent or not.

The Vaibhāṣika claim, on the other hand, was meant to explain their conviction that some of the discourses that some schools claimed to be the Buddha's were not actually his—the Perfection of Wisdom sūtras, for example. This would explain why the Tibetan textbooks on the various Indian Buddhist tenet systems claim that the schools of the Hīnayāna believed that all the Buddha's teachings were definitive—the Mahāyāna sūtras, for them, did not need "interpretation." They needed rejection as the word of the Buddha. Understood this way, the Vaibhāṣikas were not talking about a division within the Buddha's teachings of which were literal and which were not, requiring interpretation in order to bring them in line with his ultimate truth. Such a distinction they made by contrasting *nītārtha* with *neyārtha*. Instead, they were making a division within all the discourses that anyone had called "Buddha's discourses," and saying that some of them were definitive—that is, authoritatively the Buddha's—and some of them were not, a distinction they made by contrasting *nītārtha* with *anītārtha*.

Vasumitra also reported that the "reformed" Mahāsaṃghikas—the Bahuśrutīyas—held that some of the Buddha's discourses were *nītārtha* and some of them were *neyārtha* because they believed that their elders among the Mahāsaṃghikas had preserved only the "superficial meaning" of the sūtras and had neglected the "profound meaning." He also reported that another early Buddhist school, the Kaukuṭikas ("critics"), believed that only the *abhidharma*—and not the *sūtra* or the *vinaya*—was reliable, for only the *abhidharma* "contained the actual instructions of the Buddha." Nevertheless, the sparsity of information now available about the early Buddhist schools makes it impossible to be certain of the precise way in which sectarians used these terms in their debates.

One school for which considerable material on this subject still exists, of course, is the Theravāda. It maintained (and still does) a scriptural division between *nitattha* and *neyyattha* suttas and preserves the canonical justification for it in the *Aṅguttara-nikāya*: "There are these two who misrepresent the Tathāgata. Which two? He who represents a *sutta* of indirect meaning (*neyyattha*) as a *sutta* of direct meaning (*nitattha*) and he who represents a *sutta* of direct meaning as a *sutta* of indirect meaning."

The Theravāda *Kathāvatthu* and its commentary describe a dispute between the Theravādins and the Andhakas—quite possibly the southern branch of the Mahāsaṃghikas. The Andhakas held that even though all of the Buddha's actions and speech were really supramundane (Pali *lokuttara*, Skt. *lokottara*), some were perceived as mundane (Pali *lokiya*, Skt. *laukika*). The Theravādins opposed this. They, like their Hīnayāna colleagues the Sarvāstivādins, regarded the teaching the Buddha expressed in his sermon at Varanasi where he first turned the wheel of the doctrine and preached the four noble truths, to be the highest teaching, the standard against which all his other teachings were measured. And they held that sūtras in which the entities named were ultimately true were sūtras of literal meaning, definitive sūtras. Those whose language was figurative or that named entities that were not ultimately real were sūtras whose meaning had to be interpreted or inferred.

In the Mahāsaṃghika School, by contrast, all of the particular teachings collected in the canon were merely conventional (*saṃvṛti*) and were not the Buddha's final teaching. "His final teaching, the ultimate meaning (*paramārtha*) of his teaching, is 'beyond words.'" The Buddha, therefore, "turned the wheel of the doctrine" in everything he said or did, whether or not the real significance of it—how it related to the ultimate—was immediately apparent.

The Quest for Interpretive Clarity

The Theravādins' *Milinda Pañha* is a compendium of Buddhist apologetics in which the Buddhist monk Nāgasena answers questions put to him by the Greco-Bactrian King Menander about apparent contradictions in the sūtras. Nāgasena often resolves these contradictions by denying the literal sense of one of the sūtras. For example, some scriptures say the Buddha told his disciples that they were free to abrogate any of the minor rules of the monastic discipline after he passed away. Menander notes this and also observes that the Buddha said that he "taught the rules with insight," which means that they should be true for all times and places, and thus not subject to revision.

Nāgasena resolves this contradiction by denying the literal meaning of the former sūtra, which ostensibly allows changing the discipline, and by affirming the literal meaning of the latter. He says that the sūtra in which the Buddha said that the monks could abrogate the rules was an example of his testing his disciples to see if they were intelligent enough not to do it. In the same say, says Nāgasena, a king might tell his sons to divide up his kingdom after he dies in order to test their maturity, but they would nevertheless fail his trust if they actually followed his instructions.

The Pali canon records that the Buddha refused to answer some questions. These "unanswerable" (Pali *avyākata*, "inexpressible," "unspeakable") questions, such as, "Does the Tathāgata exist after death or not?" and, "Is the world eternal or not?" were avoided because they had no edifying answer or were framed improperly and were therefore conducive only to endless quarreling. Instead, the Buddha's disciples were to be concerned with the practical and certain problem of suffering and how to relieve this suffering; this was the religious path.

The search for answers to other questions was to be given up. The subjects were slippery; they "did not have only one face" (Pali *anekāṃsika*). On the other hand, the Buddha's doctrine outlining the four noble truths "had one face" (Pali *ekāṃsika*). Questions that could not be settled were to be avoided. Instead, the disciples were to turn their attention to the clear and straightforward way, described by the Buddha, that led to nirvāṇa, the release from suffering. A teacher had a duty to avoid or eliminate ambiguity and prevarication and a duty to say what he knew plainly and fully. The Buddha contrasted his own teaching to that of a "closed-fisted teacher," who holds back teachings and refuses to tell what he knows.

The Theravāda compilers of the *abhidhamma* sought clarity by purifying and analyzing the scriptures. The "unanswerable" questions, from this perspective, became riddles to be solved, and the Buddha was a master of discrimination who could figure out the solutions, but who would not enlighten certain dull worldly souls who could not have followed him without becoming confused. He gave these people simple stories and parables and did not address such subtle questions as the ultimate nature of the world. His "open-handed" policy of teaching, therefore, did not mean that he taught everything to everyone. Even though he is compassionate toward all, he still edits what he says to them, giving his listeners what will benefit them, just as a farmer sows his seed differently on different types of soil.

The most intelligent disciples, like Śāriputra, could set to work on the scriptures using their analytical abilities, in order to uncover a full, systematic explanation of the world. They could discover the unifying patterns that resolved contradictions, brought order to confusion, clarity to equivocation, and consistency to anomaly. The aim of analysis was to purify language and the faculty of understanding by discriminating and defining the correct range and use of terms.

What seemed at first to be a paradox or a contradiction in the scriptures could be shown to be a case in which different senses of a term are confused. An interpreter could sort out such confusion through discriminating analysis in the same way that a pun could be explained. The interpreter's task was to elaborate the definitions of terms ever more fully, in order to make explicit all the different senses of a word and, by doing this, to distinguish terms that could be used without equivocation; in short, to construct a philosophical language. A teacher or an interpreter of the Buddha's teachings could best reveal the truth by clearing up confusion. This is reflected in the *abhidhamma* search for the ultimate and simple constituents of the universe.

Interpretation, as the Theravāda School has practiced it, has as its goal the deciphering of equivocal language. It resolved the confusion in ordinary discourse, which resembled the confusion of categories present in figurative speech. An example of this interpretive method was the Theravādins' use of the *yamaka* or "doubled" figure of speech, in which a part of a verse or a word, "specified either as to length or position or both [was] repeated within the confines of the same verse, usually in such a way that the meaning of the two readings [was] different." As ordinarily used by Indian poets, the *yamaka* was a kind of wordplay in which one presented words or phrases that initially seemed similar but which a reader or hearer could later distinguish as having different meanings. The essence of the *yamaka's* poetic or humorous effect lay in a shifting of reference within a single word or concatenation of sounds that might be interpreted in more than one way.

The ancient Theravādins, however, did not use the *yamaka* in order to confuse categories, but, as if they were explaining a joke, to lay out all the different uses of technical terms, distinguishing one from the other. And like an earnest explanation of a joke, such a terminological exposition appears, even to contemporary Theravādin apologists, to be overzealous and tedious. Nyanatiloka Thera, in his *Guide through the Abhidhamma-piṭaka,* for example, writes of the *yamaka* collection preserved in the Pali canon that it seems as though it was "composed for examination purposes, or to get versed in answering sophistical and ambiguous or captious questions on all the manifold doctrines and technical terms of Buddhist philosophy."[73]

Contemporary Theravādin commentator Yakupitiyage Karunadasa gives an example of the *yamaka*: "Question: Is *sota* the *sotāyatana* (the organ of hearing)? Answer: (Yes, but not always, e.g.,) *taṅhāsota* (the stream of craving) is (also) *sota* but not *sotāyatana.*" To which Karunadasa comments, with a final note of exasperation:

> Here, both *sotāyatana,* the organ of hearing, and *taṅhāsota,* the stream of craving, are called "*sota*" because it occurs in both words—although of course *sota* in *sotāyatana* is different in meaning from *sota* in *taṅhāsota.* In the former it means "ear" and in the latter "stream." And, it is precisely in order to point out this difference that the whole catechism is set forth.[74]

The *yamaka* was used to distinguish the range of application of terms, to distinguish figurative from technical senses, and to specify different meanings for words that sounded the same. It requires the "checking" (*samyandana*) of terms, distinguishing technical terms basic to the system from figurative terms that are not part of the system.

A similar method for the exposition of the scriptures in the Theravādin text the *Peṭakopadeṣa* and its redacted successor, the *Netti-pakaraṇa*, deals with the summary of the doctrine and its short presentation in homilies. These texts provide a method that avoids distortion of the scriptures' meanings in their paraphrase. The method is essentially an *abhidhamma* analysis in which the terms of a text and their meanings are located on a map of *abhidhamma* categories. This constitutes, briefly, the entire duty of the expositor. The text explains various techniques for aligning a scriptural passage with the *abhidhamma* categories.

One such technique has the interpreter seek the "qualities" or "characteristics" (Pali *lakkhaṇa*) of the terms or objects mentioned in the sūtra being considered. These are the qualities embedded in the *abhidhamma* lists or in the lists of the Buddha's most important teachings, such as the thirty-seven "limbs of enlightenment" (Pali *bojjaṅga*) or other lists. Another technique involves positing the opposites of terms in the scripture in order to find the sought-after qualities. These techniques were motivated in part by a wish to have the expositor avoid deviating from the norm.

This method of exegesis makes it clear that the ultimate truth is prosaic, not poetic, and straightforward, not ambiguous. The interpreter had to chop up parables, analogies, similes, hyperbole, puns, and other figures of speech and their components and list them without confusion, just as a meditator had to mentally cut up the complex structures of the world. Grammarians, Buddhas, scriptural interpreters—they were all analysts and elucidators, masters of separating and sorting prodigious masses of confusing information.

In a scriptural passage preserved in the Chinese version of the canon, the Buddha adopts a similar pedagogical method when he interprets his own doctrine. Non-Buddhist interlopers in the monastic assembly attempt to catch him in a contradiction by posing metaphysical questions to him. The Buddha, being a master dialectician and discriminator, avoids contradiction by clarifying terms and discriminating their different senses to show that his statements do not actually contradict one another.[75]

His initial replies to their questions seem paradoxical, which only increases their perplexity, but he then eliminates the contradiction when he gives them the key to interpret his statements. For example, he resolves a seeming contradiction by explaining how, in one place, the word *nirvāṇa* has a different meaning from what it has in another place. Again, as if he were solving a riddle, he asserts that, "the world exists and the world does not exist," which puts his questioners in a quandary until he shows how the word *exist* can be glossed to reveal two different meanings. He shows that *existence* and *nonexistence* in the statement, "The universe is existent and nonexistent" do not form a contradiction. He does this by treating the term *universe* as a class name, and by understanding *existence* and *nonexistence* as synonyms for *birth* and *death.* This results in the simple assertion that there is both birth and death in the universe. He resolves paradoxes by discriminating different senses of terms that apparently contradict each other. He defines and distinguishes terms that had been confused, allowing his disciples to discern what is true from what is false.[76]

With such logical tools as the Theravādins' *yamaka* and the translation of poetic or even ordinary prose narrative discourse into the language of the *abhidhamma* categories as in the *Netti-pakaraṇa,* ambiguous, figurative, and contradictory speech was dissected and translated into the nonprevaricating and normative language of the highest teachings. The Theravādins' drive to achieve standardization and unambiguous clarity in the expression of doctrine indicates their assumption that ultimately, reality is consistent, rational, and described by terms or categories that do not overlap. Consequently, they went about their scriptural interpretation—as well as their metaphysics—much as the Mīmāṃsakas and Grammarians went about their systematic grammatical analysis of language, and to a similar conservative end—to bring what was ambiguous or deviant into line with a clearly defined and unchanging set of normative terms or categories. Theravādin exegetes and philosophers worked with the principle that under analysis, complex terms, objects, and teachings became simpler and clearer. Parts were distinguished from one another and could then be recognized in their true simple natures. It is an atomistic worldview, in which the components of the world maintain their discreteness. The Vaibhāṣikas shared that worldview.

Another worldview was incipient, however, from early on within Buddhism. The *Dhammapada* describes a "fool" who inverts the values of the mundane world, the arena of human affairs, the endless round of fortune. One who renounces the values of that world, reorders his or her life, and becomes a Buddhist mendicant is reckoned a fool by the world but is actually wise from a more profound point of view. The *Dhammapada* describes the man of the world as the true fool. The hint of a suggestion here is that the world may not be as simple as it seems. Being straightforward and plain might not always be a virtue. It might, instead, be actually foolish.

The Mahāyāna scripture the *Vimalakīrti Nirdeśa* promotes "foolishness." The world that is turned upside down by the one who appears to be a fool—but who is truly wise—is not merely the conventional world that values money over virtue. It is the conventional world of common sense, of ordinary cause and effect, and of the ordinary, established expectations of those Buddhists and non-Buddhists alike who have not perceived the ultimate truth of emptiness. In this scripture, the understanding of a carousing layman, Vimalakīrti, is placed above that of the Buddha's renowned disciple Śāriputra—the expert in *abhidharma* analysis. Śāriputra is nonplussed when he is confronted with an inversion of the natural order of things. A wonder-working goddess instructs him in the nature of reality, not only by switching categories on him in a series of linguistic acrobatics, but by continually switching her bodily appearance with that of Śāriputra and back again. One lesson from this is that one who appears to say or do foolish things may be pretending to act in that way in order to instruct those who can discern the significance of the pretense. The Buddha, too, having actually been enlightened for eons, according to the Mahāyāna, was putting on a show in acting out his worldly life. In this, he was pretending to be less exalted than he actually was. He was "conforming to the world" out of compassion for others who needed a practical demonstration of how to achieve happiness. He did this out of kindness in order to teach others and not in order to accomplish anything for himself.

The Buddha, by this logic, employs pretense as the most direct and clearest and most pointedly adapted expression of teaching about the complex nature of the world. The composer of the *Vimalakīrti Nirdeśa* worked with the principle that the more things were analyzed, the more complex they became. One part could not be isolated from any other. Things could become their own opposites. Figurative language, which could point to many things simultaneously, was a truer reflection of the complex universes in a single atom than a systematic *abhidharma* exposition. The difference in style and worldview (about conventional and ultimate truths) between the atomizing Vaibhāṣikas and the Mahāyāna is profound. Nevertheless, the doctrine of the two truths, in every Buddhist school, expresses the distinction between the real nature of the world as it is and the conceptualizations that we create and with which we encrust and distort that world. One is ultimate. The other is merely conventional.

Two Truths

Statements or Objects? Existent or Nonexistent?

EARLY *abhidharma* lists contain not only what their compilers considered to have been the Buddha's most important teachings, but also contain enumerations of what they believed really existed in the world. In the *abhidharma,* they subjected the world to analysis in order to isolate its constituents or elements. The Buddha was said to have described these elements in several different ways. One was in the list of the five "aggregates" (*skandha*). Another was in the list of the twelve "sources" or "spheres" (*āyatana*) and another was in the list of the eighteen "constituents" or "elements" (*dhātu*).

The Hīnayāna practitioners of the *abhidharma* analysis saw these categories in a variety of ways. The Sarvāstivādins, for example, saw them as having real counterparts, and developed a complex atomic theory to explain how the world was compounded from the ultimate elements that were named in their list of phenomena (*dharma*). They also divided consciousness into its constituents, and further atomized it into moments of consciousness. They saw their *abhidharma* as a kind of periodic table of elements. The Theravādins, on the other hand, while not altogether denying an atomic interpretation of the entities in the *abhidharma* lists, also saw at least some of them—the four elements of earth, water, fire, and wind—as tendencies. They saw some of the categories in these lists primarily as intensities or forces that could manifest as distinct phenomena by dominating their surroundings.[77]

The *abhidharma* phenomenology did not include such things as humans, trees, or clouds in its inventory of the universe; rather, all things were reduced to their fundamental—and therefore ultimate—constituents.[78] The terms that were the category names referred to things that truly existed. Language that used these terms was true philosophical language because its terms had ultimately real referents. The referents of other terms or "conventions" (*saṃvṛti, vyavahāra*), such as *pot*, were ultimately nonexistent, for it was only the mind that isolated them and gave them identities. They were "imputations" (*prajñapti*).[79] The Sarvāstivādins thus believed that language that referred to such things as pots (or humans or trees or clouds) was similar to language that referred to other things—imaginary things. Such language included metaphor and figuration, which could not be taken literally.

Buddhism's central doctrine is that of selflessness (*nairātmya*): The most damaging fiction that the mind constructs and mistakes as real is the self (*ātman*). For the Vaibhāṣikas, this meant that the person (*pudgala*) was simply something imputed to the collection of its constituents.[80] It could not withstand analysis and, as a result, could not be ultimately real. When one looked among the ultimate constituents of the world, there was no self among them.

The Theravādins' *Milinda Pañha*, following an argument used in the canon itself, presented the same idea. In the text, the monk Nāgasena compares the person to a chariot: when the various parts of the chariot are combined, we perceive a chariot, yet when we search among the parts, we cannot find the chariot. The same is true of the person. It is only something imputed to the collection of its constituents. The constituents alone are ultimately real. Nāgasena says that "Nāgasena" is only a name, only a designation, and that "I" is merely a convention (Pali *sammuti*), not an ultimate (Pali *paramattha*).[81] Becoming enlightened about selflessness, in this view, therefore means mentally eliminating the ghost of a self or soul or person in one's perception of the causal machinery of the world. The Vaibhāṣikas' *Mahāvibhāṣā* expresses a similar idea. It states:

> [Agents,] like the person who is born and who dies, exist conventionally (*saṃvṛti-sat*); the law of birth and death exists ultimately (*paramārtha-sat*). The person who enters and leaves *samādhi* [that is, meditation] exists conventionally; the

> *samādhi* that is being entered and left exists ultimately. The agent of [action] and the receiver of [the consequences of that action] exist conventionally; but action, its ripening and fruit exist ultimately . . . a tree, for example, is an imputation [but] the four elements . . . are substantial (*dravya*) entities.[82]

Despite the Buddha's advocacy of selflessness, however, some passages in the sūtras seemed to contradict this. The clearest example was the statement in the *Aṅguttara-nikāya* in which the Buddha said there was "one person . . . who was born out of compassion for the world, for the profit, welfare and happiness of gods and humans," and that this "one person" was a Tathāgata, a "fully enlightened one," that is to say, the Buddha himself.[83]

How can one reconcile this with the doctrine of selflessness? The Theravādin Buddhaghosa's commentary on this sūtra says that the expression "one person" is "conventional speech" (*sammuti-kathā*), not "ultimate speech (*paramattha-kathā*). Here, the Buddha was speaking figuratively when he referred to "one person." Buddhaghosa says that the Buddha had two teachings—"conventional teachings" (*sammuti-desanā*) and "ultimate teachings" (*paramattha-desanā*):

> Thus, "person" (*puggala*), "being" (*satta*), "woman" (*itthi*), "man" (*purisa*), "warrior" (*khattiya*), "Brahmin" (*brāhmaṇa*), "god" (*deva*), "Māra" (*Māra*), etc. are conventional teachings. "Impermanence" (*anicca*), "suffering" (*dukkha*), "selfless" (*anatta*), "aggregates" (*khandha*), "constituents" (*dhātu*), "sources" (*āyatana*), "foundations of mindfulness" (*satipatthāna*), and so on, are ultimate teachings.
>
> Thus, the Blessed One gives the conventional teachings to those who, having heard the teaching in terms of the conventional, are able to understand these distinctions, having penetrated the meaning, having got rid of obscurity, and he gives the ultimate teachings to those who, having heard the teaching in terms of the ultimate, are able to understand the distinctions, having penetrated the meaning, having got rid of obscurity.

The following is a simile: For example, a teacher might have mastered the languages of various countries, so that when that teacher explains the meaning of the Vedas to those who speak Tamil language, then, knowing that, he translates their meaning into Tamil. Elsewhere, he might speak in the language of Andhra, and thus, when young people meet this clever and intelligent teacher, they acquire knowledge very quickly.

The Blessed Buddha is like such a teacher, for he modifies his teaching. The canon is like the Vedas. The teacher's proficiency in various countries' languages is like [the Buddha's] proficiency in the conventional and the ultimate (*sammuti-paramattha*). The languages of the young men's various countries are like the ways to receive the teaching and gain understanding by means of the conventional and the ultimate. As the teacher translated into Tamil and so on, so the Blessed One makes known the teachings by means of the conventional and the ultimate. Thus it was said that:

> The fully awakened excellent one proclaimed two truths—conventional and ultimate (*sammutiṃ paramatthañ ca*)—no third is known. Conventional expression (*saṃketa-vacanam*) is the truth (*saccam*) in terms of worldly conventions (*loka-sammuti*); ultimate expression (*paramattha-vacanam*) is the truth in terms of the real nature (*bhūta*) of phenomena (*dhamma*). Thus, our friend, the protector of the world, who is skilled in speaking, said that one does not lie [merely] by speaking in conventions.[84]

The first section of the Theravādins' *Kathāvatthu* is devoted to trying to convict the Buddhist Saṃmitīya-Vātsīputrīya School of the claim that "the 'person' is known in the sense of a real and ultimate fact" (*saccikattha-paramatthena*).[85] The Saṃmitīya-Vātsīputrīyas scandalized other schools of Buddhism with their position on the nature of the person. Although they believed that the person was not an ultimate, they gave more ontological status to the person than the other schools' interpretations of the doctrine of selflessness would allow. According to Theravāda sources, the

Saṃmitīyas held that even though the person existed as an imputation based on the aggregates and was in a relationship with them that could not be expressed as being the same or different from them, the person was a permanent entity that passed from existence to existence. The Theravādins believed that the Saṃmitīyas must therefore argue that the person was a "real and ultimate fact."[86] The Theravādins, on the other hand, were made to argue that not only was the person merely a mentally constructed fabrication superimposed over what actually existed—that is, its constituents—but that even these constituents were impermanent.

At one point in this debate in the *Kathāvatthu*, the Theravādin debater compares the Buddha's use of the term *person* to his use of other terms, which the Theravādin cites, according to the *Kathāvatthu*'s commentary, in order to "show that meaning does not always accord with the form of what is said."[87] These other terms include such things as *butter jar*, for the reason that no one "can make a jar out of butter." *Oil jar*, *milk pail*, and *water pot* are also listed, for similar reasons. These are treated as oblique or metaphorical forms, as distinguished from a term such as *gold jar*, which is not misleading (as opposed, perhaps, to *gold-jar*) since "a gold jar is made of gold." The expression *a meal provided in perpetuity*—referring to the fact that a lay person could pledge to provide food for a monk on a permanent basis—is submitted to a similar criticism; for, in fact, "a meal instituted in perpetuity by charity is not eternal and permanent as is nirvāṇa."

From this perspective, the goal of an interpretation of the Buddha's truth was to unravel his indirect language, to spell out what he may have merely suggested, or to disentangle what he had really meant from the figures of speech he had used. He had used parables or similes in order to teach those who could not have understood him if he had spoken plainly. His discourses were full of such language, just as they seemed to be full of anomalies and contradictions, for the sūtras contained the teaching in which he had dressed up or toned down his meaning, to accord with his audience. The systematized lists of clarified technical terms in the *abhidharma*, on the other hand, constituted his real teaching because they reflected his own thought and intention. The *abhidharma* was his ultimate teaching, expressed directly, without the oblique language he used in the sūtras.

The Theravāda preserves an ancient tradition in connecting the term *sammuti* ("convention") to the collection of sūtras in general, and the term *paramattha-dhamma* ("ultimate doctrine") to the *abhidharma* collection. That tradition considers the *abhidharma* to be a systematic exposition of the sūtras, adding nothing novel. The difference is thought to be one of arrangement and treatment—looking at the same material (the world) at a different level of magnification, as it were, or from a different point of view. The sūtras explained the world in "everyday language" (*vohara-vacana*), while the *abhidharma* explained it in philosophical, technical, "ultimate language" (*paramattha-vacana*). The sūtras referred to people, places, and things, while the *abhidharma* referred to mental and physical phenomena that were ultimately real but were nevertheless "only of momentary duration, arising and passing away every moment."[88]

Saṃghabhadra (sixth century C.E.), a Vaibhāṣika writer and critic of Vasubandhu's *Abhidharmakośa*, described the relationship between the two truths and the Buddha's teaching:

> The teaching that speaks of certain persons, of cities, gardens, forests, and so on belongs to the conventional, but because that teaching is meant to indicate a true meaning and is not intended to deceive others, it is called "truth." The teaching that speaks of the aggregates, constituents, sources, and so on belongs to the ultimate. It has as its aim the explication of the true character of phenomena. It destroys the notions of unity, of solidity, of a being. It exposes reality (*tattva*). Therefore it is called "truth." The teaching of the four truths causes men to confront reality; it is of the ultimate.[89]

Certain statements could be reckoned as "conventional truths," therefore, because they referred to things that were true or real objects, but only true or real in the limited sense that, under analysis, they could be broken up into other constituents. Certain other statements could be reckoned as "ultimate truths" because they referred to things that were true or real objects even under analysis. "Truths," then, were not just statements or language or speech, but the objects to which the statements referred. Some of those objects were of a different order than others.

One way to explain the two truths, therefore—or at least the two truths as a categorization of objects—is to say that things that exist conventionally—like the person—do not, in reality, exist, and things that exist ultimately do, in reality, exist. We could then make the following categories of things in the world:

Existents (*sat*):

1. *Paramārtha-sat* "ultimate existents" (for example, the *skandha* "aggregates")

Nonexistents (*asat*):

2. *Saṃvṛti-sat* "(only) conventional existents" (for example, persons and pots)
3. The totally nonexistent (for example, the horns of a rabbit—a classic Buddhist example)[90]

But this categorization is not sufficient. One simple way to explain why is to point out that the last part of the compound *saṃvṛti-sat* ("conventional existent") is *sat* "existent." There is something wrong with putting it in the same general category as totally "nonexistent" (*asat*) things like the horns of a rabbit or—invoking other Buddhist textbook examples—a cloak made of turtle hair, or the son of a barren woman. These things do not exist at all, so they are very different from persons and pots, which do exist conventionally.

We have three things and only two baskets to put them in. The three things are *paramārtha-sat*, *saṃvṛti-sat*, and *asat*. We can categorize the three differently than we did above. In this way, persons and pots have more in common with the *skandha* than they do with the horns of a rabbit insofar as both pots and *skandha* do exist, although in different ways:

Existents (*sat*):

1. *Paramārtha-sat* (*skandha*, etc.)
2. *Saṃvṛti-sat* (persons, pots, etc.)

Nonexistents (*asat*)

3. *Asat* (horns of a rabbit, etc.)

The difference in these two categorizations is that of viewpoint, or the frame of reference for the large categories of "existents" and "nonexistents." The frame of reference for the first is an "ultimate" one, for the second it is a merely "conventional" one.

The Vaibhāṣikas maintained a "two-basket" categorization scheme. They chose the second of these above, in which both the conventional and the ultimate were put into the basket of "existents." By choosing this one, they avoided the "extreme of annihilation (or nihilism)" that would threaten their scheme if they had chosen the first one above, which would have put them in the position of saying that the conventionally existent things of the world do not, in fact, exist.[91] Nevertheless, if they had given two baskets, one marked "exists" and the other marked "does not exist," to an "ultimate" sorter, that sorter could not find either conventional things to throw into the "exists" basket, or for that matter, anything at all for throwing into the "does not exist" basket, since something that "does not exist" does not exist and, therefore, could not be found for throwing into either basket.

This is an unstable situation. One scholar has attributed this to the conflicting demands to account for the fact that the person exists (conventionally) as well as the fact that it does not exist (ultimately): "The distinction between *satyas* reflects . . . the logical requirements of resolving a tension between two epistemological and ontological positions; firstly, that all intentional objects of consciousness are given existential status, and secondly, that the requirements of analytical certainty necessitate a more fundamental ontological status for some existents than others."[92]

The goal of knowledge, for the Theravādins, therefore, is not precisely the elimination of the ghost of a person in the causal machinery of the world. Although, from among the schools considered here, they came closest to conceiving of the situation in these terms, describing the "person" as a mechanical marionette with no reality of its own, they did not deny the validity and value of the conventional world of persons and pots.

Two Truths and Four Truths

Saṃghabhadra said that in his time some people treated the doctrine of the two truths as if it concerned the teachings and some people treated e two truths as objects, such as pots and atoms.[93] He could have said the me thing about the doctrine of four truths—the four noble truths. The ibhāṣikas (but not the Theravādins) aligned the categories of the two ıths with those of the four truths, and thereby also made it possible to eat the four truths as primarily objects, just as some treated the two ıths.

In this way, the "truth of suffering" (*duḥkha-satya*), which most have derstood as referring to a verbal proposition—that is, to the Buddha's tement that existence is suffering—could be treated in a way that is bet- r translated as "true sufferings." These are objects—the mental and ysical aggregates produced by contaminated actions and afflictions. ıe "truth of the origin (of suffering)" was transformed into "true ori- ns," that is, the contaminated actions and the affliction of ignorance nsidered as causes of "true sufferings." The "truth of the cessation (of ffering)" became "true cessations," which included, for example, nir- ṇa, as well as the absence of some spiritual affliction or misconception. ıe "truth of the path (leading to the cessation of suffering)" became ue paths," the individual "path consciousness," that is the moment of nsciousness that results in the achievement of a "true cessation."

The various explanations that the early schools gave of how the two ıths aligned with the four truths focused both on the ways in which the ıddha expressed his teaching, as well as the objects to which his teach- g referred. The Vaibhāṣikas' *Vibhāṣā* sets out various positions without king them to specific persons or schools:

> According to one opinion about the four truths, the first two (sufferings and origins) are conventional truths because all the mundane things immediately perceived in the world—man, woman, going, resting, pot, cloth, etc.—are included in the first two of the four truths. The last two truths (cessations and paths) are ultimate truths because the supramundane (*lokottara*) reality (*tattva*) and the supramundane qualities (*guṇa*) are included in those two truths.
>
> According to another opinion, the first three truths (sufferings, origins, and cessations) are conventional truths. There are some mundane things in the first two, as was just indicated. As

> for true cessation, the Buddha said that it was like a city, like a palace, like the other shore. Insofar as worldly designations refer to true cessation, it follows that the true cessation also is called a conventional truth. Only the true path is the ultimate truth because one does not find there any worldly designations.
>
> According to another opinion, the four truths are all conventional truths. For the first three truths, it is as was indicated above: they are conventional truths because mundane things are found in them. The true path also includes some mundane things because the Buddha taught the true path by applying to it the words *śramaṇa* and *brāhmaṇa.* Only the principle, "All things are empty and without a self," is the ultimate truth because in emptiness and selflessness all mundane things lose their designations.[94]

The *Vibhāṣā* next recounts an opinion that each of the four truths includes both conventional and ultimate truths because each of the four can be explained using mundane language and using more precise, philosophical language as well, in terms of the sixteen attributes of the four noble truths.[95]

The explanations of "true sufferings" that use worldly terms such as *man, woman, going, resting, pot,* and *cloth* are included in conventional truths. The explanations of "true sufferings" in terms of their four attributes are included in ultimate truths. The four attributes of true sufferings are impermanence (*anitya*), suffering (*duḥkha*), emptiness (*śūnya*), and selflessness (*anātmaka*).

In a similar way, "true origins" can be explained in the same mundane terms, or in terms of their four attributes. These four attributes are: being a cause (*hetu*), being an origin (*samudaya*), being capable of strong production (*prabhāva*), and being a condition (*pratyaya*).

The Buddha also used mundane terms when explaining "true cessations," comparing a true cessation to a city, a palace, a garden, a forest, and to the other shore; but true cessations can also be explained in terms of their four attributes: cessation (*nirodha*), pacification (*śānta*), auspiciousness (*praṇīta*), and being the definite emergence (from saṃsāra) (*niḥsaraṇa*).

Finally, the Buddha used mundane terms when explaining "true paths," comparing a true path to a raft, a mountain of stone, a stairway, a dike, a flower, and water; but he also explained them in terms of their four attributes: being a path (*mārga*), being suitable (*nyāya*), being an achievement (*pratipad*), and a deliverance (*nairyānika*).

This position, which aligns both conventional and ultimate truths with each of the four noble truths, is that of the Vaibhāṣikas in the *Vibhāṣā* as well as the *Mahāvibhāṣā* and Saṃghabhadra's *Samaya-pradīpika*, which he wrote to clarify the orthodox Vaibhāṣika doctrine free of the Sautrāntika bias he believed had crept into Vasubandhu's *Abhidharmakośa*.

Saṃghabhadra also cited and argued against the position of Śrīlāta, who held that three of the four noble truths—sufferings, origins, and paths—included both conventional and ultimate truths since their designations (*prajñapti*) were conventional truths, while their actual substances (*bhūta-dravya*), which serve as the support of their designation, were ultimate truths.[96] Śrīlāta maintained that a true cessation, because its "own nature" (*svabhāva*) was inexpressible, could not be aligned with either conventional or ultimate truths.

One of the reasons Saṃghabhadra gave for disagreeing with this was that Śrīlāta considered a true cessation, that is, nirvāṇa, to be "inexpressible" (*avyakṛta*). For Saṃghabhadra, if something was inexpressible, it was a conventional truth. But nirvāṇa definitely was not a conventional truth. It was, considered in itself, the ultimate truth. Again, the idea of something's being inexpressible derived from the Buddha's refusal to answer categorically such questions as, "Does the Tathāgata exist or not after death?" and "Is life the same thing as the body?" The answers to these questions were inexpressible. For Saṃghabhadra, a Vaibhāṣika, this meant that the entities asked about in these questions, such as the Tathāgata, were conventional truths. They were inexpressible because one could not say either that they were identical with or separate from their constituents. This was also the case with a pot, for example, which was neither identical with, nor separate from, its parts.

One other possible way exists to align the four truths with the two truths. All four truths could be ultimate truth in that they constitute the Buddha's highest teaching, which is the way to salvation, or in that they formed the content of the Buddha's first (and therefore most fundamental) sermon. The knowledge of this sort of truth is very different from that of the "medical requisites of a patron," for example, which is certainly useful, or knowing the shortest way to town, but this latter type of knowledge does not have the same ultimate value as knowledge of the four truths. It is, instead, "conventional knowledge" (*sammuti-ñānam*).[97] This interpretation, which contrasts conventional knowledge to the higher soteriological knowledge of the four truths, is also suggested by the categories of knowledge in the Vaibhāṣikas' early text, the *Abhidharma-hṛdaya*, as well as the chapter on knowledge (*jñāna*) in Vasubandhu's *Abhidharmakośa*.[98]

The Vaibhāṣika School and the Two Truths

The Vaibhāṣikas tried to develop a purified philosophical language that meant what it said, that denoted real entities. To do this, they had to figure out exactly what real entities there were in the world. These were things that were impervious either to the attempt to separate them physically or mentally. Such things existed ultimately. Their existence was not dependent on mental imputation. They existed in their own right, apart from the mind that looked at the pure momentary flux of the universe and saw larger patterns. The ultimates included the smallest atoms and the smallest moments of consciousness. Ultimates were also such things as form (*rūpa*), because no matter how much a form was broken apart, a form was the result.[99] There were, however, different categories of form and of consciousness, such as the aggregates, the constituents, and the sources.

One sort of language, the conventional, referred to the gross entities named in ordinary discourse which, after a close analysis, could not be maintained as ultimately real. The other sort of language referred to the entities that constituted the real structure of the world, free of mental superimposition. This was stated by the Sarvāstivādin Vasumitra (first century B.C.E.): "That which is said in conformity with the world (*lokānurodhena*) is called conventional; that which is said in conformity with the nobles (*ārya*) is called ultimate."[100] He also said, "To speak of living beings (*sattva*), of a pot, of cloth, and other things, expressions (*vyavahāra*) produced by a thought that is not false—that is conventional truth. To speak of causality (*pratyāyata*), of production by reason of conditions, and of other principles, expressions produced by a thought that is not false—that is ultimate truth."[101]

The Vaibhāṣika author of the *Abhidharmadīpa* gave his own definitions of the two truths, which made ultimates the unvarying entities that underlay conventional things:

> That which, in the ultimate sense, is always grasped in its own being (*svabhāva*) and never abandons its own nature (*svātman*) and which is related to an object that is not created by any person (*apauruṣeya-viṣaya*) and that conveys it to discriminating knowledge (*viṣiṣṭa-jñāna*) exists ultimately. Moreover, in contrast to the numerous ultimately true things, that which is indicated with the form of a designation (*prajñapti*) for the sake of conventional usage (*vyavahārārtham*) exists conventionally, such as a pot, a cloth, a forest, a person.[102]

His reference to "objects that are not created by any person" is the Vaibhāṣikas' way of speaking about the objects in their list of *dharma* ("phenomena").

Among the seventy-five *dharma* named in the *Abhidharmakośa*, a group of fourteen cannot be classed in either the category of forms (*rūpa*), minds (*citta*), mental factors (*caitasikas*), or unconditioned things (*asaṃskṛta*).[103] These fourteen miscellaneous *dharma* are grouped under the name *compositional factors not associated with the mind* (*citta-viprayukta-saṃskāra*). Three of them are "the 'forces' that impart significance to words, sentences, and letters."[104] These are the *word* (*nāma-kāya*, literally, "name-body," in the sense of a totality or collection that constitutes a word), the *sentence* (*pada-kāya*), and the *letter* (*vyañjana-kāya*).

Both the Vaibhāṣikas and the Sautrāntikas agreed that sound (*śabda*) was material. It was made up of sound atoms that came into being accompanied by other atoms. Sounds or words therefore were classed as form aggregates (*rūpa-skandha*), and were classed in their *dharma* list under forms. But the Vaibhāṣikas, considering the nature of the word of Buddha (*Buddha-vacana*), decided that it was not only of the nature of verbal sound (*vāk*), which they classed as a sound that was a material form, but was also of the nature of *nāma* (literally, "name"), one of the non-material categories of *dharma*, as opposed to the material or form category. Undoubtedly, this was meant to exalt the nature of the Buddha's word above ordinary speech. Vasumitra's commentary on the *Abhidharmadīpa* cited a phrase in scripture as support for the Vaibhāṣikas' contention that the Buddha's word has a dual nature:

> While the Lord lives, his words are of the nature of speech (*vāk*) as well as of the nature of *nāma* respectively, in a secondary and primary sense. After his final nirvāṇa, however, his words are only of the nature of *nāma* and not of *vāk*. For the Lord of the Sages had a "heavenly sound" not comparable to any mundane speech.[105]

Yaśomitra also described a Vaibhāṣika view that the Buddha's word was "the arrangement in regular order . . . of the *nāma-kāya*, the *pada-kāya*, and the *vyañjana-kāya*," which placed it in a different category from other sounds.[106]

The Vaibhāṣikas, as represented in the *Abhidharmakośa*, also held that verbal sound, in itself, cannot convey any meaning, but rather it operates on the name, and then the name conveys the meaning.[107] The *Abhidharmadīpa* states that names are accompanied by meanings, and the *Abhidharmakośa* states that names are what produce ideas (*saṃjñā*).[108] The meaning of a word is therefore not in its material sound, but in the immaterial forces that convey the meaning (and that are "non-associated compositional factors")—the *nāma-kāya*, the *pada-kāya*, and the *vyañjana- kāya*.

The author of the *Abhidharmadīpa* also subdivides the *nāma-kāya* into two categories—those "not created by any person" (*apauruṣeya*) and those that are "worldly" (*laukika*). The *Abhidharmadīpa* says that the *nāma-kāya* that convey or denote (*abhidhānā*) the constituents, the sources, and the aggregates are those that are not created by any person, and that only a Buddha perceives these. The *Abhidharmadīpa* also uses this fact to explain an unattributed statement that "the *nāma-pada-vyañjana-kāya* appear when the Tathāgatas appear in the world."[109] This relates to the *Abhidharmadīpa*'s definition of ultimate truth in that it is the constituents, the sources, and the aggregates that are "not created by any person" and that are therefore ultimately true. This aspect—that certain things were not created by any person—makes this similar to the Theravādin idea that certain names are "spontaneously arisen" (*opapatika-nāman*), referring to things that name themselves, as it were, or are born with their names attached—like feeling (*vedanā*), one of the aggregates and therefore a basic element.

This veers toward the Mīmāṃsakas' and Grammarians' thoughts on the eternality of the Vedas, which they also regarded as "not created by any person," the same phrase they used to describe the relationship between the Vedic word and its meaning.[110] The innate meanings they ascribed to the words of the Vedas led the Mīmāṃsakas to postulate the word, that is, sound, as a separate source of valid cognition (*pramāṇa*), revealed by hearing (*śruti*), apart from other sources such as inference and direct cognition.[111] Modern scholars are still uncertain whether the Mīmāṃsakas influenced the Vaibhāṣikas on this issue or whether the influence was in the opposite direction.[112]

The Vaibhāṣikas' notion that the Buddha's word was, in a primary sense, different from the sounds he uttered, perplexed the Sautrāntikas, who, as reported in the *Abhidharmakośa*, argued against the idea that a *nāma-kāya*, the conveyor of meaning, could arise at the end of speaking the phonemes, one by one, that make up a word.[113] The meaning of the *nāma-kāya*, they pointed out, had to embrace all of the phonemes together, but the first ones pronounced were already nonexistent by the time those at the end of the word were pronounced. This was a damaging criticism because the Vaibhāṣikas held that the *nāma-kāya* was an impermanent—that is, instantaneous—thing being a non-associated compositional factor, and could not arise bit by bit, forming itself as the word was pronounced, but had to arise all at once at the end of the word's pronunciation.

The Sautrāntikas, who criticized the Vaibhāṣikas' claim that an impermanent thing, the *nāma-kāya*, could convey the meaning of a word, perhaps ultimately passed on to Tibet, through the logicians Dignāga and Dharmakīrti, a different approach to the problem. The function that the Vaibhāṣikas attributed to the *nāma-kāya*—conveying the meaning of a word to the mind—is similar to that attributed by the Tibetan monastic writers to something called the "meaning generality" (Tib. *don spyi*, Skt. *artha-sāmānya*). This meaning generality conveys the meaning of a word, as opposed to the collection of sounds that make up the word, the "sound generality" (Tib. *sgra spyi*, Skt. *śabda-sāmānya*). If one does not know the meaning of a word, the pronunciation of the sound merely produces a sound generality—just a pattern of sound—without an image of what it means—the meaning generality.[114] Dignāga's and Dharmakīrti's meaning generality and the sound generality, however, unlike the Vaibhāṣikas' *nāma-kāya*, are permanent. They do not disintegrate moment by moment, as does the impermanent referent object to which the image is linked.

The Tibetan Gelukpa Gönchok Jigmay Wangpo wrote, "The word of Buddha and the treatises are both asserted by the Vaibhāṣikas to be entities that are collections of letters, stems, and words. They are accepted as the generic images of sounds and as non-associated compositional factors. Therefore, one wonders whether in this system form and non-associated compositional factors are not mutually exclusive."[115] Actually, write his commentators, "he is wondering whether the Vaibhāṣikas would say that the sounds heard from the mouth of Buddha are not the word of Buddha."[116] Nevertheless, when the Vaibhāṣikas used the term *generic image of sounds* or *sound generality* (*śabda-sāmānya*), they may have meant something that did not itself have the nature of sound, and was therefore not a form but was impermanent. This would have made it unlike the *sound generality* or *meaning generality* later distinguished by the Sautrāntikas, which were permanent.

The primary source for understanding the Vaibhāṣikas' ideas of the ultimate and the conventional is Vasubandhu's *Abhidharmakośa*, which contains this verse:

> If the awareness of something does not operate after
>   that thing
> Is physically broken up or separated by the mind into
>   other things,
> It exists conventionally, like a pot or water;
> Others exist ultimately.[117]

Vasubandhu's own commentary on this verse offered examples of things that exist ultimately, taken from the Vaibhāṣikas' categories of phenomena (*dharma*). These phenomena are in five categories—minds (*citta*), mental factors (*caitasikas*), forms (*rūpa*), factors not associated with the mind (*citta-viprayukta*), and unconditioned or uncomposed phenomena (*asaṃskṛta*). The examples of ultimates that Vasubandhu gave are form and one of the mental factors—feeling (*vedanā*).[118]

According to the *Abhidharmakośa*, something that exists conventionally, like a pot, is no longer apprehended as such after it is broken apart. The same is true for water, although water can be broken apart into its components only by the mind, which can isolate such things as its odor and taste. Pūrṇavardhana, an Indian commentator on the *Abhidharmakośa*, wrote that Vasubandhu's two examples of conventional things, pot and water, refer to categories of things that can be physically broken apart and things that can be broken apart only by the mind. But, he wrote, they can also be understood to refer to other ways to categorize conventional truths—that is, conventional objects. They may be taken as examples of conventional objects that manifest a definite shape, like a pot, and of conventional objects that have no definite shape but are merely collections of particles, like water.[119]

Pūrṇavardhana wrote that the category of conventional objects that have a definite shape could also be regarded as what we might call the category of "second-order" conventional objects, that is, those conventional objects that are themselves constructed of components that are also conventional objects. A pot, for example, has a handle, a bottom, sides, an inside and an outside, and these things are not ultimates themselves. Following Pūrṇavardhana, the category of conventional objects that are merely collections of particles may be regarded as what we might call "first-order" conventional objects, that is, those conventional objects, like water, that are directly constructed of substances, that is, ultimate particles, and have no parts grosser than these.

This distinction between "first-order" and "second-order" conventional truths did not originate with Pūrṇavardhana, for Saṃghabhadra had already used it. In his *Nyāyānusāra*, Saṃghabhadra divided the category of "existents" (*sat*) into two divisions—the substantially existent (*dravya-sat*) and the imputedly existent (*prajñapti-sat*).[120] He then wrote that the category of the imputedly existent consists of two kinds of things. They are those things that depend or are based upon the substantially existent (these imputedly existent things are our "first-order" conventional truths), and also those things that depend or are based upon other imputedly existent things (which describes our "second-order" conventional truths). The distinction between the substantially existent and the imputedly existent corresponded to the distinction between ultimate truths (*paramārtha-satya*) and conventional truths (*saṃvṛti-satya*).[121]

Saṃghabhadra said that an existent (*sat*) is that which "produces an awareness (*buddhi*) that characterizes an object." He also said that when the awareness is produced corresponding to some one thing without depending on other things, that thing substantially exists. He gave, as examples of things that substantially exist, form and feeling. He said that when the awareness is produced corresponding to some one thing that depends on other things, that thing imputedly exists. He gave as examples, a pot and an army.

His examples of a pot and an army are relatively easier to understand as examples of first- and second-order conventional things than Vasubandhu's examples of water and a pot. Saṃghabhadra wrote:

> What imputedly exists is . . . of two sorts—that which depends on things which exist in themselves, and that which depends on things existing by imputation. Examples are, respectively, a pot (designated to [a collection of] atoms), and an army (designated to [a collection of] persons, who are [themselves] designated to [collections of] the five aggregates).[122]

His explanation made a pot a first-order conventional object, while Vasubandhu's example of a pot was understood by Pūrṇavardhana to refer to a second-order conventional object. But however the examples of these categories are handled, it does not change the fact that the Vaibhāṣikas maintained that "ultimately exists" (*paramārtha-sat*) was synonymous with "substantially exists" (*dravya-sat*) and that "conventionally exists" (*saṃvṛti-sat*) was synonymous with "imputedly exists" (*prajñapti-sat*).

The non-Buddhist grammarian Patañjali's *Mahābhāṣya* stated that, "a substance is the substratum of qualities" (*dravya* also denotes the grammatical entity, the substantive).[123] Patañjali defined substance as "that which does not lose its essence or reality even though other things, qualities, come to inhere in it."[124] In his *Vākyapadīya*, Bhartṛhari maintained that a substance was permanent and that one of its synonyms was "self" (*ātman*).[125]

Generally, non-Buddhists used the term *substance* to refer to the permanent constituents that formed the bedrock of the phenomenal world. Buddhists, however, including the Vaibhāṣikas, held that nothing had a "self" and that all substances were impermanent. As a corollary, Buddhists held that there were no permanent, substantially existent universals, which, it was said, informed particulars and gave them their identities. Nevertheless, even though the Vaibhāṣikas held that substances were impermanent and disintegrated in each moment, they connected the notion of substance with that of ultimate truth, and other Buddhist schools viewed this with some suspicion.

The Gelukpas, in explaining the Vaibhāṣikas' tenets, say that the Vaibhāṣikas held that while some things substantially existed and were therefore ultimately existent, they also held that everything that existed, even conventionally, was substantially established (*dravya-siddha*). No such distinction between the substantially existent and the substantially established exists in the *Abhidharmakośa* or in Saṃghabhadra's works. If first- and second-order conventional objects, however, are progressively built up from fundamental components that substantially exist, then the Vaibhāṣikas may have held that even conventional things, like pots, were at least built up from the substantially existent. In this way, the term *substantially established* could mean *established upon the substantially existent.*

Other Buddhists, however, regarded connecting even conventional truth with the notion of substance as a gross reification of conventional truth. Ngawang Belden, for example, stated:

> The Vaibhāṣikas assert that all phenomena are substantially established. For, as they are excessively involved in searching for the imputed objects, they would not know how to posit something to exist if it were merely imputed to other factors (Tib. *chos*) and were not established as a separate, autonomous, substantial entity.[126]

Other schools may have technically accepted the idea that the basis of all existent things—even imputedly existent ones—was the substantially existent. Something about the phrase "substantially established," however, seemed to them to improperly reify the imputedly existent. In Ngawang Belden's passage above, for example, applying the phrase "substantially established" to something connotes that it is "established as a separate, autonomous, substantial entity." The sources do not provide evidence for why it necessarily meant this, but the absence of the term *dravya-siddha* in the *Abhidharmakośa* and in Saṃghabhadra's *Samaya-pradīpika* and *Nyāyānusāra* suggests that the term may have become critical only in later debates. A detailed search of the later Indian commentaries on the *Abhidharmakośa* might turn up a definition of "substantially established" that implies such things' independent, autonomous natures, as the Tibetan commentaries say it does.

Saṃghabhadra, in the *Samaya-pradīpika*, quoted the Sthavira sectarian Śrīlāta's definitions of the two truths, which also relied on the idea of substance:

> That which exists in many substances is conventional; that which exists in a single substance is ultimate. Moreover, if, when one divides it, the thing (*dharma*) in question loses its original name, it is conventional; if it does not lose it, it is ultimate.[127]

Saṃghabhadra had objections to this definition. For example, he objected to the word "single" because it could mean "isolated" from other substances, which, in fact, a substance never is, because it always exists in concert with others. But Śrīlāta's definitions are consonant with Dharmakīrti's Sautrāntika idea that generally characterized things (*sāmānya-lakṣaṇa*) were merely conventional, while uniquely or specifically characterized things (*sva-lakṣaṇa*) were ultimates.

Saṃghabhadra did point out, however, at least one other difference between his own Vaibhāṣika position and Śrīlāta's, which was, in this respect as well, like that of the Sautrāntikas, whose positions were detailed in the *Abhidharmakośa*:

> For the Sthavira [that is, Śrīlāta], the aggregates (*skandha*) are only conventional, while the real substances (*bhūta-dravya*) that serve as the support for the designation of the aggregates are ultimates. This is also the case with the sources (*āyatana*), while the constituents (*dhātu*) are [always] ultimates.[128]

The Vaibhāṣikas, as the *Abhidharmakośa* made clear, regarded the aggregates, the sources, and the constituents (or "types") as ultimates, and held that even one atom of "form," for example, qualified as a "form aggregate" (*rūpa-skandha*). On the other hand, the Sautrāntikas, as described in the *Abhidharmakośa* (and by Śrīlāta) held that, of these three categories, only the constituents (*dhātu*) were ultimates. They pointed out that the word *aggregate* (*skandha*) was commonly glossed as *pile* (*rāśi*) in the scriptures, and that *sources* (*āyatana*) was glossed as the *doors* (*dvāra*) of consciousness. Unless these were misnomers, they said, then when only one particle of them was present, no matter what sort of particle it was, it could not function as a "pile," and it could not form a "door." Only a constituent (*dhātu*) remained true to its name when there was only one of them present, and for this reason, the constituents alone, and not the aggregates or sources, were ultimates. The Sautrāntikas, therefore, regarded the aggregates and sources as existing merely by imputation, that is, as merely conventionally true. As a corollary to this, they held that more than one particle of "form" was needed to qualify as a "form aggregate."

According to the Vaibhāṣikas, there were two kinds of particles or atoms. First, there was the "atom" or "particle" (*aṇu*). Second, this "atom" was constituted of a minimum of eight "smallest particles" (*paramāṇu*), which were indivisible. Sometimes, both the "particle" and the "smallest particle" were called "smallest particle" (*paramāṇu*), and when that was done, a distinction was maintained by referring to the larger of the two as a "conglomerate atom" (*saṃghāta-paramāṇu*) and the smaller one as a "substance atom" (*dravya-paramāṇu*).

The substance atom never exists in isolation. Generally, it comes into being in combination with at least seven others, all of which arise in the same moment and pass away in the same moment. Each of these eight substance atoms, which compose the conglomerate atom, consist of one of each of the four primary elements (earth, water, fire, and wind) and of one of each of four of the secondary elements (visible form, odor, taste, and touch arisen from the elements).

The exceptions to this general description of the conglomerate atom as having eight atoms within it occur when there is an additional atom of sound—a kind of matter—appended to it, for a total of nine atoms, or when there is another atom of a sense faculty—also made of matter—of some kind, for a possible total of ten atoms.[129] These numbers apply to the lowest of the realms of saṃsāra, the "Desire Realm" (*Kāma-Dhātu*), which is where we live. There are two other realms—the "Form Realm" (*Rūpa-Dhātu*) and the "Formless Realm" (*Ārūpya-Dhātu*), each one subtler than the previous. Accordingly, the matter in the Form Realm, for example, is lighter and less complex than that in the Desire Realm. The conglomerate atom in the Form Realm lacks atoms of odor and taste. Thus the conglomerate atoms of the Form Realm are composed of six, seven, or eight substance atoms, rather than eight, nine, or ten, as they are in the Desire Realm.[130]

The conglomerate atoms cannot be physically separated. The smaller atoms that compose them never exist in isolation.[131] When "water" is given as an example of a conventional truth, this refers to water considered as the massed stuff that flows in rivers and that is collected in pots. Its components, actually its qualities, such as form (but no discernable shape), its odor, its taste, can be picked out by the mind. But a single conglomerate atom of water cannot be divided. Although it is a conglomerate, none of the substance atoms that constitute it can be said to lie in a particular direction from any of the others. The conglomerate atoms, therefore, are "directionally partless," just as the substance atoms are. Since the conglomerate atom's components cannot be said to be in one place or another in relation to the other components, these components (the substance atoms) are the same size as the conglomerate atom they compose.

Both the substance atom and the conglomerate atom, therefore, are equally indivisible and are both ultimates. (Note that "water" considered as the gross, physical flowing mass is a conventionality, that a single conglomerate atom of water is an ultimate, and that this "water" is distinguished from the "water" that is one of the four primary elements and one of the eight smallest substances atoms that compose a conglomerate atom. This "water" substance atom is considered one of the form atoms that are ultimates.)[132]

An atom even lacks the quality of "impenetrability" or "resistance" (*pratighāta*), which is the quality of form that gives it spatial extension.[133] This quality makes a form an obstacle. Without it, that form's place would be occupied by another form. According to Yaśomitra, the Vaibhāṣikas held that the substance atoms were without this quality of resistance or impenetrability because they wished to claim that they were without parts. This is presumably because the quality of resistance entailed another quality, that of "covering" (*avarṇa-lakṣaṇa*) or extension.

In the *Abhidharmakośa*, the Sautrāntikas point out to the Vaibhāṣikas that if it were the case that the substance atoms lacked this quality of resistance, then they did not qualify as form (*rūpa*). This is because the fundamental characteristic of form, according to the definition (in the *Abhidharmakośa*), is that it has resistance (*sapratighāta*). The Vaibhāṣikas reply, "Certainly the smallest particle is exempt from having 'formness' (*rūpana*). But a form that is a smallest particle never exists in an isolated state. In a conglomerate state, being in a conglomerate (*saṃghātastha*), it is properly resistant."[134] Consequently, they held that these substance atoms were devoid of parts, "partless" (*niravayavat*).

In the *Abhidharmakośa* and in Yaśomitra's commentary, the Sautrāntikas—who refused to accept that conglomerate atoms were without parts—then pressed the Vaibhāṣikas. They asked them how it could be that if none of the substance atoms were extended in space and if none of them offered any resistance, how could many together do this?[135] How could one put together many atoms that took up no space and obtain something with any extension at all? But, according to Hsüan Tsang's *Vijñaptimātratāsiddhi*, the Sautrāntikas were themselves pressed by Cittamātrin opponents to explain how they could accept these atoms as ultimates if they held that they were in fact divisible into smaller parts.[136]

Saṃghabhadra explicitly divided the category of the substantially existent into two subcategories—that which possesses only its own being (*sasvabhāvamātra*), and that which (also) possesses an active function (*sakāritra*). This division figured into the Vaibhāṣikas' assertion that even past and future objects substantially exist. According to Saṃghabhadra's category division, past and future objects possessed their own beings, but present objects possessed, in addition, an active function.[137]

Ngawang Belden wrote that the Vaibhāṣikas maintained two different kinds of ultimates—conditioned (*saṃskṛta)* and unconditioned (*asaṃskṛta*). The examples given of conditioned ultimates are the five aggregates (*skandha*). The unconditioned ultimates are space (*ākāśa*), analytical cessations (*pratisaṃkhyā-nirodha*, the cessation of some mental phenomenon brought about by the active elimination of it by mental analysis), and non-analytical cessations (*apratisaṃkhyā-nirodha*, the cessation of something simply due to the lack of conditions necessary to produce it, and not due to any active elimination of it).[138]

Saṃghabhadra himself does not explicitly state this division of ultimates, but he does make "substantially existent" synonymous with "ultimately existent," and he also holds that the aggregates substantially exist. He also argues against the Sautrāntikas who held that the three unconditioned things do not substantially exist, but only exist imputedly.[139]

The debates, reported in the *Abhidharmakośa* and in Saṃghabhadra's works, between the Vaibhāṣikas and the Sautrāntikas about the unconditioned illuminate both schools' attempts to come up with an ontology reflecting the Buddha's "middle way" and not forcing them to reify existence or totally deny it.

The Vaibhāṣikas, as we have seen, distinguished the existent (*sat*) from the nonexistent (*asat*) and divided the category of existents into substantially existent (*dravya-sat*) and imputedly existent (*prajñapti-sat*). They held that *existent* (*sat*, derived from the verb *as* "be") was synonymous with *thing* (*bhāva*, derived from a different verb meaning "be"—*bhū*).[140] For the Vaibhāṣikas, therefore, *bhāva* meant "existent" just as *sat* did.[141] For them, everything that was *sat* was *bhāva*, and vice versa. These terms' negatives were also synonymous—*asat* "nonexistent" was the same as *abhāva* "nonexistent."

They also held that the unconditioned, including space and nirvāṇa (an analytical cessation) were substantially existent. It followed then that they were both *sat* and *bhāva*. Saṃghabhadra wrote that the Sautrāntikas, in contrast, asserted that the three unconditioned things were not substantially existent "because they are not separate entities like form, feeling, and so on."[142] He wrote that, according to the Sautrāntikas, space, for example, is simply the absence of obstructive contact, and that "when people, in their ignorance, do not encounter something providing resistance, they say, 'that is space.'" Saṃghabhadra responded as a Vaibhāṣika:

> You say that space is simply the absence of obstructive contact, and that the absence of obstructive contact is named "space." I agree with that because space *is* the absence of obstructive contact. But by what argument do you establish that what is named "space" is *only* the absence of obstructive contact and is not a distinct thing (*bhāvāntara*)?[143]

His argument here was with the way the Sautrāntikas used the word *bhāva*. For them, *bhāva* was not synonymous with *sat* and could not be translated as "existent." Instead, *bhāva* was synonymous with *anitya* (the "impermanent") and *saṃskṛta* (the "conditioned"), and the unconditioned—including space and nirvāṇa—were neither impermanent nor conditioned. The Sautrāntikas held, therefore, that the unconditioned were *abhāva* (literally, "non-existent"), by which they meant something like "not a functioning (or impermanent) thing." But because the Vaibhāṣikas equated *sat* with *bhāva*, they understood the Sautrāntikas' argument to imply that the unconditioned, like nirvāṇa, were nonexistent (*asat*). For the Vaibhāṣikas, *abhāva* did not mean "non-thing," it meant "nothing." Saṃghabhadra argued this point in particular, against the Sautrāntikas' assertion that nirvāṇa was *abhāva*, which implied to him that they had fallen into nihilism:

> If nirvāṇa, in its nature, is totally nonexistent (*abhāva-svabhāva*), why would it be said in sūtra that it is the first (*agra*) among all the *dharma*, the *saṃskṛta* and the *asaṃskṛta*? Why would it give the name *dharma* to some nonexistent thing? Among *dharma*—which have their own characteristics (*sva-lakṣaṇa*)—one says that there are, among them, good and

> not so good, but it is inconceivable that one should speak thus of the horns of a rabbit or of flowers [that grow in the] sky [that is, of totally nonexistent things]. We therefore hold as certain that nirvāṇa is a distinct thing (*bhāvāntara*), which, possessing its own being, is called a *dharma*, and that this *dharma*, from among all the other *dharma*, is of a superior essence. It is proven that nirvāṇa substantially exists. Moreover, the Blessed One explicitly says that nirvāṇa "is" (*asti*). For *sūtra* says, "O monks, know that it is unborn; if it were not unborn, there would not be any abandonment of the suffering of birth and death. But, as the unborn is . . .[144]

The Sautrāntikas, however, did not equate *abhāva* with *asat*. They believed that there were some things that could be said to be *abhāva* but not *asat*. Saṃghabhadra reported the Sautrāntikas' response to his criticism, as given above:

> We do not say that nirvāṇa does not exist at all (*asat*). But there is a way in which we say that it does exist (*sat*). It is similar to the way in which one says, "There is a nonexistence (of the sound) prior to the sound; there is a nonexistence (of the sound) after the sound" (. . .*asti śabdasya paścad abhāvaḥ*). It is impossible to say of a nonexistent (*asat*) that it exists (*bhāva*). Therefore the word "is" (*asti*) is employed without implying the idea of existence [that is, "thingness," *bhāva*].[145]

In other words, the unconditioned could be predicated as *abhāva* without entailing that they were totally nonexistent. Consequently, a thing like space could be predicated as a "mere absence," as *abhāva*, without implying its nonexistence (*asat*). This would have been impossible for the Vaibhāṣikas, who held that not only was space an "absence," but also that it was by no means a "mere" absence, but rather was a distinct *bhāva*.

Ngawang Belden considered the difference between the Vaibhāṣikas and the Sautrāntikas about whether or not the unconditioned were "mere absences" and whether or not the unconditioned were *bhāva*. He used terminology that was apparently developed by the Sautrāntika logicians

Dignāga and Dharmakīrti.[146] He wrote that the Sautrāntikas held that the unconditioned were "non-affirming negatives" (*prasajya-pratiṣedha*), that is, things that exist and are yet mere absences that do not suggest some positive existent. Gönchok Jigmay Wangbo, the Gelukpa writer on Indian Buddhist tenets, also used the same terminology in describing the Vaibhāṣika system: "They do not accept the existence of non-affirming negatives because they consider all negatives to be, necessarily, affirming-negatives (*paryyudāsa-pratiṣedha*)."[147]

The debates on the nature of atoms and on modes of existence illustrate the difficulties that Vaibhāṣika and Sautrāntika sectarians encountered in trying to accommodate the gross, conventional, physical world—there things always have a multiplicity of qualities, parts, aspects, or relationships—to a view that these gross objects were built up from—and thus divisible into—things that were, at least in some sense, ultimately simple.

The attempt to isolate such ultimately simple things also lay behind a dispute between the Vaibhāṣikas and the Sautrāntikas recorded in the *Abhidharmakośa* on whether or not shape (*saṃsthāna*) existed ultimately or imputedly. The Vaibhāṣikas maintained that it was an ultimate. It was classed as a *kāya-vijñapti* (literally, "making known of the body"). This "disposition" or "shape" was visible, and it could be perceived independently of color. It was invariably present when there were forms present.[148]

The Sautrāntikas, on the other hand, did not accept that shape was an ultimate. In the *Abhidharmakośa*, they argued that shape was a derivative characteristic that comes into being from the mere arrangement of particles, such as color particles, which they maintained were real particles (agreeing with the Vaibhāṣikas on this), and which were part of the conglomerate atom.[149]

Ngawang Belden also described a debate, among the various proponents of Vaibhāṣika, Sautrāntika, and Cittamātra tenets, with regard to sense perception. His description cursorily dealt with many issues of importance to these schools. These included: How does one explain that each particle in a composite of particles can, somehow, appear to a sense consciousness? When one perceives a composite, does a single sense consciousness perceive the whole composite or its individual parts? Are the perceiving subject and its perceived object simultaneous or do they occur one after the other? Does an image of a perceived object travel to the sense consciousness of the subject that perceives it?[150]

Briefly, in this debate, Ngawang Belden gave the following views as those of the Vaibhāṣikas: The subject and object in sense perception are simultaneous. The object does not "cast a likeness of itself" or any sort of intermediary representation toward the subject, because the subject perceives its object nakedly. The perceiving subject and the perceived object are different substantial entities. A single particle cannot be perceived by itself. It cannot be the "object of activity" (Tib. *spyod yul*) of a sense consciousness. But when a mass of particles is present, the mass is perceived (making the mass the "object of activity" of a sense consciousness). In addition, each particle in that mass serves as a condition for the perception of the mass, or in other words, for the mass' appearance to the subject. This makes each particle in a composite an "observed-object-condition" (Skt. *ālambana-pratyaya*), a condition that provides for the sense consciousness observing its object. An illustration from Jetāri in this regard is that of the hair in a horse's tail. A single hair from the tail cannot be seen at a distance, but because all the hairs in the tail are present, the mass of hair—the tail—is perceived and each hair necessarily contributes to this perception.

Ngawang Belden also explained here that the Sautrāntikas, on the other hand, believed that the subject and the object were different substantial entities and in a cause and effect relationship with each other, and so could not be simultaneous. The perceived object had to have come into being first, and only after this did a subject perceive it. Because they were different substantial entities, their relationship had to develop over time, rather than simultaneously.

According to Ngawang Belden and his sources, the Sautrāntikas also held that the object "cast a likeness of itself" (Tib. *rang 'dra'i rnam pa gtong*) to the subject, which perceived this likeness. The likeness served as an intermediate factor between the different entities of the object and the subject. The Sautrāntikas shared this idea of the object's "likeness" with the Cittamātrins. The question that both the Sautrāntikas and the Cittamātrins tried to answer was whether this likeness more properly belonged to the entity of the subject or that of the object. According to Ngawang Belden, the Sautrāntikas held that even though the object and subject were different substantial entities, the "likeness" of the object was one substantial entity with the object itself. It was for this reason, they said, that the sense consciousness could be said to clearly perceive the object, even though it was actually the "likeness" that it encountered.

The Cittamātrins, using a sort of rule of parsimony, believed they could do away altogether with the need to assert the existence of external objects that were different substantial entities from the subjects that perceived them. They held that the subject and the object were the same substantial entity and that they both came into being as a result of the maturing of mental predispositions planted in the person's mental continuum at an earlier time. They still described the perceptual event as involving a subject and object, and a "likeness" of the object, but they claimed that both object and "likeness" were not different substantial entities from the consciousness that was the perceiving subject.

Therefore, because the Cittamātrins retained the perceptual mechanism, even though it was ultimately produced by mental predispositions, they were still faced with the problem of describing the relationship between the components of the perceptual event. Was the likeness cast by the object precisely the same substantial entity as the perceiving subject, or was it merely "not different" from that subject? To this question, there were two different opinions among the Cittamātrins. The "True Aspectarians" (Tib. *rnam bden pa*) held that the likeness was actually one substantial entity with the perceiving consciousness, but the "False Aspectarians" (*rnam rdzun pa*) held that, although they were not different substantial entities, the likeness was not exactly one substantial entity with the perceiving consciousness.[151]

A Gelukpa Presentation of the Two Truths in the "Śrāvaka" Schools

A TRANSLATION OF THE FIRST SECTION OF NGAWANG BELDEN'S

An Explanation of the Meaning of the Conventional and the Ultimate in the Four Tenet Systems, The Spring Cuckoo's Song of Good Explanations

The Book and Its Author

NGAWANG BELDEN was a Mongolian, born in the area of Khardal Zasag in Tseten Khan Prefecture in 1797 C.E.[152] He entered the religious life and took the first of the four degrees of monastic vows under Gelsang Töndrup (sKal-bzang Don-grub), who gave him the name Belden Nyima (dPal-ldan Nyi-ma). Subsequently, he went to Urga—later called Ulan Bataar—where he took the second and third degrees of monastic vows under the supervision of the scholar and abbot Ngawang Keydrup (Ngag-dbang mKhas-grub) who gave him the name Ngawang Belden. Through this, he was admitted to the Ganden Monastery in Urga in 1831, where he studied the sūtra and tantra systems of the Gelukpas in the College of Drashi Chöpel. He attained the Mongolian scholastic rank of Gapju in that same year.[153]

When he was forty years old, the Manchu Imperial House made him the Chöjay of Urga, which high post he occupied until 1847. During this period he traveled to Tibet for the Gongdzok (*dgong-rdzogs*) ceremony for the Fourth Jetsün Damba, who was reckoned as the reincarnation of the Buddhist historian Tāranātha.

After returning to Urga, he gave up the post of Chöjay and spent the remainder of his life traveling to various places in China and Inner Mongolia, preaching Buddhism and composing many books, most of which are included in the five-volume collection of his works printed at Urga. He became well known as an author both in Mongolia and in Tibet.[154]

The following translation is the first section of his work on the two truths, *An Explanation of the Meaning of the Conventional and the Ultimate in the Four Tenet Systems, The Spring Cuckoo's Song of Good Explanations,* which he composed in Urga in 1835.[155] It is written from the point of view of the Gelukpas, specifically of the Gomang College of the Drepung Monastery in Lhasa, as is clear from his frequent citation of Jamyang Shayba's works as authoritative evidence for doctrinal positions. In this book, the tenets of each school are first presented in a general way and then examined more carefully through challenges and responses formulated in the fashion of the syllogistic debate commonly used by Gelukpas. Although these take the form of "debates," in fact the interlocutors' positions function primarily as a means for the author to bring up what he considers to be misconceptions.

An Explanation of the Meaning of the Conventional and the Ultimate in the Four Tenet Systems, The Spring Cuckoo's Song of Good Explanations

I pay respectful homage at the feet of my lama, who is indistinguishable from the venerable Mañjuśrī.[156] (1b)

May the compassionate king of subduers, the unparalleled leader, the god of gods, bestow great virtuous blessings upon us forever.[157] He causes a rain of the profound and vast doctrine to fall, and gently issues cloud-sounds of pleasant utterances, free of error, amid the rain clouds of his Form Body, bedecked with glittering rainbows that blaze forth the splendor of his marks, which have arisen from their empowering conditions—his unobstructed wisdom and mercy—along the collected immortals' broad path, the nature of which is that of the Truth Body, free of elaboration, spontaneous and unchanging.[158] (2a)

Obeisance to the Conqueror's invincible regent [Maitreya] and to Mañjuśrī, who have reached the end of the path of the Conqueror's sons on the force of the wind of their generating the intention to bear the doctrine of the Conqueror, and who shine brightly as ornaments in the sky of the Conqueror's teaching.

Nāgārjuna and Asaṅga have well crafted the supreme golden stairway on which scholars may joyfully ascend to the great arbor of the Subduer's marvelous instruction. If their kindness had form, it would not fit in the sky.[159]

Those who support the traditions of the chariots: Āryadeva, the supreme scholar Śūra [that is, Āśvaghoṣa], Buddhapālita, Bhāvaviveka, Candrakīrti, Śāntideva, the authors of the three [Svātantrika-Mādhyamika] texts, the honorable Vimuktasena and Haribhadra, Vasubandhu, Sthiramati, Dignāga, Dharmakīrti, Devendrabuddhi, Śākyabuddhi, Suvarṇadvīpi, Ratnākaraśānti, and so on—the many scholars in the country of Superiors [India]—(2b) are a constellation of stars adorning the expanse of sky that is the Subduer's teaching.[160]

Scholars have praised the supreme of superiors, the protectors of the three lineages, and Samantabhadra and so on, as being the "transmigrators' eyes"; in accord with their own wishes, they have assumed human form as kings, ministers, translators and scholars, as well as the Elder [Atīśa], his spiritual sons, and so on.[161]

Until I attain enlightenment, may my spiritual guide be Tsongkhapa, the fruitful flower whose learnedness, holiness and goodness, in the form of a tortoise, have supported the Earth of the Conqueror's teachings, whose explanation, debate and composition, in the form of a wild boar, have suppressed the Brahmā-world of those who claim to be scholars, whose power of scripture and reasoning, the form of Rāma, has taken the lives of evil ten-necked disputants.[162]

I worship those who wear the golden crown: the two supreme spiritual sons [of Tsongkhapa—Gyaltsap and Keydrup—] and the rest, who lifted up the flow of the Ganges, the good explanations of the Protector [Tsongkhapa] as a bath for the feet of the tenth incarnation [of Viṣṇu], the teachings of the Subduer.[163]

Obeisance to [Jamyang Shayba,] the Vajra at whom Mañjuśrī smiled, who emanated a thousand rays illuminating difficult points and cleared away dark clouds of wrong conceptions by stirring up a great wind, the reasonings of refutation and proof.[164]

Who could not have faith in the successive protectors [the Dalai Lamas], propagating the lotus garden of excellent doctrine, radiating the light of learnedness, holiness and goodness, drawn in the great sky-chariot of powerful compassion? (3a)

With the crown of my head at their feet, I worship the group of dragon kings. Heralded by the spring cuckoo, their great mercy, they are spiritual friends who have kindly dressed the world of my mind in emerald-threaded summer garments, their good explanations.

O spiritual guide, you are the immortal leader in whom there is seen nothing that does not equal [Sarasvatī,] the daughter of Brahmā, with a voice of a thousand graces, you are the scholar who has command, in song, over all the meanings of the texts.[165]

May the father and mother, the lord of wisdom Mañjuśrī [and Sarasvatī], brilliantly blazing like the white crystal side of Mount Meru, resplendent with the luster of a hundred thousand moons, bestow on me the accomplishments of mind and speech.

Relying on the best helmsmen, the spiritual guides, the supreme scholars, I will now bring forth here, from the ocean of the multitude of scholars' textual systems, a beryl having eight facets, supreme topics of scholarship, so that I may fulfill the hopes of those who wish to become wise.[166]

Though this [truth] is not something desired nowadays by those [self-styled] "excellent ones" who are "free of attachment," who see the gold of good explanations and the dross of bad explanations as equal, discerning helmsmen should hold fast to it in their hearts.

Those seeking the treasure house of meaning should set this on top of the banner of discrimination and not be oppressed by those who acquire a multitude of sinful friends who wag their tongues in the obscurity of errant speech. (3b)

About this, the foremost one, the great being [Tsongkhapa] says [in his work *In Praise of Dependent-Arising*]:

> All of your various teachings
> Are based solely on, and begin from, dependent-arising
> And exist for the sake of our passing beyond sorrow;
> You have nothing that does not tend toward peace.[167]

Accordingly, dependent-arising (*pratītya-samutpāda*) is the very topic into which all the eighty-four thousand ways to approach the doctrine flow and descend. These doctrines were spoken by the teacher, the king of subduers, as antidotes to the eighty-four thousand ways to act out afflictions that transmigrators adopt. Moreover, the glorious protector and superior Nāgārjuna says [in the *Treatise on the Middle Way (Mūlamadhyamaka Kārikā)*]:

> Doctrines taught by the Buddhas
> Depend entirely on the two truths:
> Worldly, conventional truths,
> And ultimate truths.[168]

The *Superior Sūtra on the Meditative Stabilization in Which Suchness is Definitely Revealed (Tattvanirdeśa-samādhi Sūtra)* says:

> The Knower of the World, without hearing about them from anyone else, has taught by means of these two truths.[169]

Thus it is said that of all the doctrines stated by the blessed Buddha, none at all deviate from teaching either the dependent-arising that consists in the class of appearances, which are conventional truths (*saṃvṛti-satya*), or the dependent-arising that consists in the class of emptinesses, which are ultimate truths (*paramārtha-satya*). Thus, the essential aim of the Conqueror's sayings and the commentaries on his thought is simply the unmistaken resolution of the status of the two truths. For that reason, the scholar kings, in concordant thought, have extensively praised this from the point of view that there is tremendous fault in not realizing the two truths, but that if one does realize them, it is very meaningful, etc. Nāgārjuna's *Treatise on the Middle Way* says:

> Those who do not thoroughly know
> The difference between those two truths
> Do not know the profound principle
> Of the Buddha's teachings.
>
> Without relying on the conventional, (4a)
> The ultimate cannot be taught;
> Without realizing the ultimate,
> Nirvāṇa is not attained.[170]

Candrakīrti's *Supplement to (Nāgārjuna's) "Treatise on the Middle Way" (Madhyamakāvatāra)* says:

> Conventional truths, which are the means, and
> Ultimate truths, which arise from the means—
> He who does not know the difference between those two
> Has entered upon an evil path due to his
> wrong conception.[171]

Jñānagarbha's *Differentiation of the Two Truths (Satyadvaya Vibhaṅga)* says:

> Those who know the difference between the two truths
> Are not obscured as to the Subduer's word;
> Amassing all the collections [of merit and wisdom],
> They proceed to complete perfection.[172]

Moreover, all the sayings of the Conqueror and the stainless treatises, which are the commentaries on his thought, just teach the means to liberate transmigrators from cyclic existence (*saṃsāra*). As was said:

> . . . And are for the sake of our passing beyond sorrow;
> You have nothing that does not tend toward peace.[173]

Even liberation from cyclic existence is not achieved by any other means than by meditation after resolving, without mistake, the ultimate status of phenomena (*dharma*).[174] As the *Sūtra on the King of Meditative Stabilizations (Samādhirāja Sūtra)* says:

> If the selflessnesses of phenomena are individually analyzed
> And one meditates on what has been individually analyzed,
> This is the cause, the effect of which is the attainment
> of nirvāṇa;
> One does not become peaceful through any other cause.[175]

The presentation of conventionalities, such as those of the aggregates (*skandha*), constituents (*dhātu*), sources (*āyatana*), the twelve branches of dependent-arising, etc., and in particular, those of predicates (*dharma*) and subjects (*dharmin*), those things to be proved (*sādhya*) and the proofs (*sādhana*), one (*eka*) and different (*bheda*), and so on, which frequently appear in the scriptures, are only stated as means to realize the ultimate status of phenomena. This accords with the earlier citations of Nāgārjuna's *Treatise on the Middle Way* and Candrakīrti's *Supplement*. Also, Bhāvaviveka's *Heart of the Middle Way (Madhyamaka Hṛdaya)* says:

To climb to the top of the palace of reality
Without the stairs of
Real conventionalities
[Is known] among the wise to be impossible.[176] (4b)

The "Chapter on Inference for Oneself" in Dharmakīrti's *Commentary on (Dignāga's) "Compendium of (Teachings on) Valid Cognition" (Pramāṇa-vārttika)* says:

All the presentations of objects proved and their proofs,
Of predicates and subjects,
As well as that of the different
And the not-different,

Are done by the Sage in order to understand the ultimate,
Depending upon such presentations,
Just as they are renowned in the world,
Without analyzing the meaning of suchness.[177]

Therefore, you should know that the non-erroneous knowledge of the two truths is the principal goal of all the scriptures and the unsurpassed means to liberate transmigrators from cyclic existence.

Not only that, but merely through taking an interest in the profound doctrine, one amasses immeasurable merit, and there are immeasurable benefits, such as [its becoming] difficult to be reborn into a bad transmigration, and the suppression of [the effects of] one's having committed even great sins, such as the five which incur immediate [retribution after death], and so on.[178] That this is so accords with the statement in Tsongkhapa's *Great Explanation of (Nāgārjuna's) "Treatise on the Middle Way"* on the meaning of the Superior Nāgārjuna's citation and explanation of the five sūtras in his *Compendium of Sūtras (Sūtra Samuccaya)*, such as the *Sūtra for the Precious Child* and the *Diamond Cutter (Vajracchedika)*.[179]

Also, there are an endless number of statements like the one in Āryadeva's *Treatise in Four Hundred Stanzas (Catuḥśataka-śāstra)*:

> Those who have little merit do not even
> Have doubt about this doctrine.
> Through merely having doubt,
> Mundane existence is torn apart.[180]

Therefore, so that I might establish predispositions in myself for the doctrine, and thinking it might help others as well whose lot is the same as mine, I will explain a little of the meaning of the two truths.

This explanation has two parts: an enumeration of the assertions of the proponents of true existence and an explanation of the two truths in the Mādhyamika system.[181]

Part One: The Proponents of True Existence

Chapter One: The System Common to the Śrāvaka Schools[182]

As for the system common to the Śrāvaka schools, (5a) Vasubandhu's *Treasury of Higher Knowledge (Abhidharmakośa)* says:

> If the awareness of something does not operate after that thing
> Is physically broken up or separated by the mind into other
> things,
> It exists conventionally, like a pot or water;
> Others exist ultimately.[183]

Also Vasubandhu's *Explanation of the "Treasury of Higher Knowledge" (Abhidharmakośa-bhāṣya)* says:

> If the awareness of something does not operate after it is physically broken up into its parts, it exists conventionally, as is the case, for example, with a pot . . .[184]

The explanation of the meaning of such statements has two parts—their general meaning and a final analysis.

General Meaning

This has two parts—conventional truths and ultimate truths.

Conventional Truths. The definition of a conventional truth (*saṃvṛti-satya*) is: A phenomenon (*dharma*) with regard to which the awareness apprehending it does not operate when [the phenomenon is physically] broken into parts or mentally separated into its components. Illustrations are a pot and water. Vasubandhu's *Treasury of Higher Knowledge* says:

> If the awareness of something does not operate after that thing
> Is physically broken up or separated by the mind into other
> things,
> It exists conventionally, like a pot or water;
> Others exist ultimately.[185]

Vasubandhu's *Explanation* says:

> If the awareness of something does not operate after it is physically broken up into its parts, it exists conventionally, as is the case, for example, with a pot. When it is physically broken up into shards, the awareness of the pot does not operate. If the awareness of something does not operate after it is separated by the mind into other phenomena, it is to be understood to exist conventionally, as is the case, for example, with water. When the mind separates out other phenomena, such as form, the awareness of water does not operate.[186]

"Conventional truth" (*saṃvṛti-satya*), the "conventionally existent" (*saṃvṛti-sat*), and the "imputedly existent" (*prajñapti-sat*) are synonymous (*ekārtha*) [that is, coextensive].

They assert that whatever is an established base (*āśrayā-siddha*) is necessarily truly established (*satya-siddha*) but is not necessarily ultimately established (*paramārtha-siddha*); and that whatever is an established base is necessarily substantially established (*dravya-siddha*) but is not necessarily substantially existent (*dravya-sat*). This is because the Vaibhāṣikas assert that all phenomena are substantially established. For, as they are excessively involved in searching for the imputed objects, they would not know how to posit something to exist if it were merely imputed to other phenomena (*dharma*) and were not established as a separate, autonomous, substantial entity.

They posit the meaning of imputed existent and substantial existent through whether or not the awareness apprehending them (5b) is caused to cease when they are physically broken or mentally separated into other things. Jamyang Shayba's *Great Exposition of Tenets* says:

> They assert that all are substantially established because they do not know how to posit something if it is merely imputed to other phenomena and does not have its own separate autonomy. Also, there is a great difference between the substantially existent and the imputedly existent because, for the most part, being substantially existent means it is ultimately established and being imputedly existent means it is conventionally established.[187]

The First Dalai Lama's *Ornament of Reasoning for (Dharmakīrti's) Works on Valid Cognition* explains this by distinguishing between that which exists as a substance (*rdzas su yod pa*) and substantial existent (*rdzas yod*).[188]

They divide conventional truths into two types—conventionalities that are shapes and conventionalities that are collections. The former are also said to be conventionalities that depend upon other [physical] conventionalities and the latter to be conventionalities that depend upon other substances. In the line ". . . like a pot or water," examples are given, respectively, of that which is destroyed by [physical] breaking and of that which is mentally destroyed; or, respectively, conventionalities that depend upon other [physical] conventionalities and conventionalities that depend upon other substances. Pūrṇavardhana's *Commentary on (Vasubandhu's) "Treasury of Higher Knowledge" (Abhidharmakośa-ṭīkā Lakṣaṇānusāriṇī)* says:

> Those which are destroyed by being [physically] broken are such things as pots. Those which are mentally destroyed are

> such things as water, for it is impossible to separate out such things as the taste of water from it, for instance, by physically breaking it up. In another way, conventionalities are of two types—conventionalities that are shapes, such as pots, and conventionalities that are collections, such as water; and for this reason, the two examples are given. Or again, the two examples given in the statement, "If the awareness of something . . . like a pot or water," indicate two types of conventionalities because existents such as pots, which exist in dependence upon the parts of the pot, are conventionalities that depend upon other [physical] conventionalities, but such things as water, (6a) which exist in dependence upon substances such as form, are conventionalities that depend upon other substances.[189]

Conventionalities that are shapes are necessarily conventionalities that are collections because they must be masses that are composed of particles. Conventionalities that are collections are not necessarily conventionalities that are shapes because conventionalities that are collections, like water, are not conventionalities that are shapes. For although the mind can separate water into its individual components such as odor and taste, the eight substances in a minute particle (*paramāṇu*) of water cannot be individually separated out. Rājaputra-Yaśomitra says:

> There is a [physical] destruction of the [conventionality] that depends upon other [physical] conventionalities, and there is also the mental separation of it into other things. As for that which depends upon other substances, there is only its mental separation into other things and no physical destruction; a minute particle cannot be separated into the eight substances that are its components.[190]

Etymology of "conventional truth" (saṃvṛti-satya). The reason for calling such things as a pot or water *saṃvṛti* is that when the shapes, such as bulbousness, or the substances such as the form, the odor, and the taste of water, have become interdependent, the statements, "A pot exists on that base," and, "Water exists on that base," are true and not false. Candrakīrti's *Clear Words (Prasannapadā)* refers to three usages of the word *saṃvṛti*—for that which obstructs [one's seeing] suchness, for the interdependent, and for the conventions of the world.[191] From among these, it [that is, the usage of *saṃvṛti* that we mean] refers to the interdependent. As for *satya*, Amarasinha's *Immortal Treasury (Amarakośa)* says:

> *Satya* is used for the true (*bden*), the good (*legs*), the existent (*yod pa*), the praised (*bsngags pa*), and that which is worthy of worship (*mchod 'os*).[192]

Here it [*satya*] must refer to the existent, or the true as opposed to the false. It is explained that *saṃvṛta* is used for the bound together (*bsdams pa*), the opened (*gdang pa*), the protected (*bskyangs pa*), the destructible (*zhom pa*), and so on. In this context, the convention (*kun rdzob*) is appropriately explained as "bound together," "destructible," and so on.

The way I have just explained the etymology (6b) of *saṃvṛti-satya* is correct, for Vasubandhu's *Explanation* says:

> Only those things are conventionally designated with those names. Therefore, when through the force of convention one says, "There is a pot," and "There is some water," one has quite simply spoken the truth and not something false, and for that reason they are conventional truths.[193]

Ultimate Truths. The definition of an ultimate truth is: A phenomenon, the awareness apprehending which is not cancelled even though it is broken or mentally separated into its individual components. Illustrations of it are directionally partless particles and partless moments of awareness. For Vasubandhu's *Treasury of Higher Knowledge* says, " . . . Others exist ultimately." Also, Vasubandhu's *Explanation* says:

> Others are ultimate truths. Something exists ultimately if the awareness of it operates even though it is physically broken or

> mentally separated into other factors, as is the case, for example, with form (*rūpa*). Even if it is physically broken up into minute particles or is mentally separated into phenomena such as its taste, the awareness of the entity of form still operates. Feelings and so on should be viewed in the same way.[194]

"Ultimate truth" (*paramārtha-satya*), the "ultimately established" (*paramārtha-siddha*), the "ultimately existent" (*paramārtha-sat*), and the "substantially existent" (*dravya-sat*) are synonymous.

Ultimate truths can be divided into two types—conditioned (*saṃskṛta*) and unconditioned (*asaṃskṛta*) ultimate truths. The former are [found among each of] the five aggregates (*skandha*). The latter are of three types—space (*ākāśa*), analytical cessations (*pratisaṃkhyā-nirodha*), and non-analytical cessations (*apratisaṃkhyā-nirodha*). Although feeling (*vedanā*), discrimination (*saṃjñā*), intentions (*cetanā*), and so on are each ultimate truths, a collection or a continuum of them is not an ultimate truth because when either a collection or a continuum is mentally separated into discrete parts, the awareness apprehending them as a collection or a continuum is necessarily cancelled. (7a) As Pūrṇavardhana's *Commentary* says:

> "Feelings and so on should be viewed in the same way" means that collections of feelings, discriminations, intentions, and so on, exist conventionally, but that each of these—feelings and so on—should be viewed as substantially existent. Why is this? Feelings substantially exist because even if feelings and so on are mentally separated, there will be an awareness of the entity of feeling. This should be applied in the same way to intentions, and so on.[195]

With respect to forms, feelings, and so on, which are ultimate truths, there is a reason for calling them "ultimate truths," because even though they may be broken up or mentally separated into discrete parts, they still exist as forms, feelings, and so on. Vasubandhu's *Explanation* says, "Since they exist ultimately, they are called 'ultimate truths.'" The way in which they exist ultimately is as was explained earlier, for Vinītabhadra's

Commentary on (Vasubandhu's) "Treasury of Higher Knowledge" (Abhidharmakośa-vṛtti Sūtrānurūpa) says:

> Something exists ultimately if the awareness of it operates even though it is physically broken or mentally separated into other phenomena.[196]

In this context, *paramārtha* means that which does not depend upon parts, and *satya* means that which is comprehended through reasoning, etc., for although an isolated particle of a substance, for instance, cannot abide without depending upon other substances, this does not contradict the fact that, without depending upon other substances, an awareness apprehending it does not operate. For although an awareness can apprehend an isolated particle of a substance, that particle can neither abide nor be produced in isolation. This is because in order for a gross form to be produced or abide, it must be produced and must abide together [in a collection of] at least six particles of substances [in the Form Realm and at least eight in the Desire Realm]. This is the meaning of the statement in Vasubandhu's *Treasury of Higher Knowledge* that says:

> In the Desire Realm, [a mass of] minute particles that
> does not have [a particle of] sound
> And that does not have [a particle of] a sense faculty
> consists of eight substances;
> One that has [a particle of] the faculty of touch—
> nine substances;
> One that has [a particle of] another sense faculty—t
> en substances.[197]

Also, the following is implied:

> In the Form Realm, a mass of minute particles that does not
> have [a particle of] a sense faculty
> And that does not have [a particle of] sound consists of six
> substances,
> Since there is neither smell nor taste in the higher realm;

> [One that has a particle of the faculty of touch consists of seven substances;
> One that has a particle of another sense faculty—eight substances.][198]

Final Analysis

First Debate

Someone says: There is no Sautrāntika who asserts [the two truths] in accord with the statement, "If the awareness of something does not operate . . .," because there are no [such Sautrāntikas] said to exist in Vasubandhu's *Explanation* or in [Yaśomitra's] commentary on it and because the Sautrāntikas' assertions accord with the statement in Dharmakīrti's *Commentary on (Dignāga's) "Compendium"*: "That which has the capacity to function ultimately . . ."[199]

Our reply: It follows that that is not correct because according to the system common to the Vaibhāṣikas and Sautrāntikas, they [the two truths] must be asserted in accord with the explanation in Vasubandhu's *Treasury of Higher Knowledge* and the Sautrāntikas Following Scripture do assert them in that way.

It is established [that according to the system common to the Vaibhāṣika and Sautrāntika systems, the two truths must be asserted in accord with the explanation in Vasubandhu's *Treasury of Higher Knowledge*] because Devendrabuddhi, in his *Commentary on the Difficult Points of (Dharmakīrti's) "Commentary on (Dignāga's) 'Compendium'" (Pramāṇavārttika Pañjikā)*, in the context of refuting the "principal" (*pradhāna*) [asserted by the Sāṃkhyas] says:

> Does it exist conventionally like water, milk, and so on, or does it exist ultimately like form, pleasure, and so on?[200]

This reason entails [that according to the system common to the Vaibhāṣikas and Sautrāntikas, the two truths must be asserted in accord with the explanation in Vasubandhu's *Treasury of Higher Knowledge*] because it is not suitable for this passage to be explaining assertions that are peculiar only to the Vaibhāṣikas.[201] Another reason is that this is said to be common to the Vaibhāṣikas and Sautrāntikas in Jamyang Shayba's *Great Exposition of Tenets.*

That [the Sautrāntikas Following Scripture assert the two truths in accordance with the explanation in Vasubandhu's *Treasury of Higher Knowledge*] is established because the Sautrāntikas following Vasubandhu's *Treasury of Higher Knowledge* assert them in that way. For the *Ornament for (Dharmakīrti's) Seven Treatises* says:

> The explanation in Vasubandhu's *Treasury of Higher Knowledge* and the presentation of the two truths by these Sautrāntikas Following Reasoning accord only in being Sautrāntika presentations, but their systems are not the same. This is because the explanation in Vasubandhu's *Treasury of Higher Knowledge* is the system of the Sautrāntikas who assert that an atom (*aṇu*) must be partless.[202]

It also says:

> Since those Sautrāntikas and these have different systems, they should not be confused.

Also, Jamyang Shayba's *Great Exposition of Tenets* says:

> According to the *Commentary on the Difficult Points, An Ornament for (Dharmakīrti's) Seven Treatises (Pramāṇavarttikā Pañjikā),* the Sautrāntikas Following Scripture and the Vaibhāṣikas assert them in accord with the *Treasury of Higher Knowledge,* but the Sautrāntikas Following Reasoning do not [assert them] in that way. The explanation is made within that framework.[203] (8a)

Second Debate

Someone says: It [absurdly] follows that the Sautrāntikas Following Scripture assert that "substantially existent" and "ultimately existent" are synonymous because [according to you] the Sautrāntikas Following Scripture agree with the Vaibhāṣikas in their assertions on the two truths.

Our reply: [That the Sautrāntikas Following Scripture agree with the Vaibhāṣikas in their assertions on the two truths] does not entail [that the Sautrāntikas Following Scripture assert that "substantially existent" and "ultimately existent" are synonymous] because, although they agree in their presentations of the two truths, there is a very great difference in the way that they assert what the substantially existent and the imputedly existent are. It is established [that although they agree in their presentations of the two truths, there is a very great difference in the way that they assert what the substantially existent and the imputedly existent are] because the Vaibhāṣikas and these Sautrāntikas differ: 1) on whether or not to assert the three unconditioned phenomena to exist substantially; 2) on whether or not to assert the aggregates to exist substantially; and also, 3) on whether or not to assert shape (*saṃsthāna*) to exist substantially.

That [they differ on whether or not to assert the three unconditioned phenomena to substantially exist] is established because the Vaibhāṣikas assert that the three unconditioned phenomena are both substantially established (*dravya-siddha*) and substantially existent (*dravya-sat*), but the Sautrāntikas do not assert them as such.

That [the Vaibhāṣikas assert that the three unconditioned phenomena are both substantially established and substantially existent] is established because the Vaibhāṣikas assert that the three unconditioned phenomena are substantially established, that they are unconditioned things (*bhāva*), and that they substantially exist. This is established because they assert: 1) that the three [unconditioned phenomena (*asaṃskṛta*)] are substantially established since they are established as separate autonomous substances; 2) that they are unconditioned because they are not produced from causes and conditions; 3) that they are things-that-have-their-own-nature (Tib. *rang bzhin gyi dgnos po*, Skt. *svabhāva-vastu*) because they are autonomous substances; 4) that they are things which are objects of observation (*ālambana-pratyaya*); 5) that they are permanent because what exists earlier exists later; and 6) that they substantially exist and ultimately exist because although they are mentally separated into their components, their entities are still apprehended by the mind.

This [six-part reason] is established because such is the case with analytical cessations, and, by extension, the other two [unconditioned phenomena—space and non-analytical cessations] are also established as such.

That by extension the other two unconditioned phenomena are also established as substantially and ultimately existent is proved through Vasubandhu's *Explanation*, which says:

> [Question:] What is this "separation"?
> [Answer:] Was it not explained earlier as an "analytical cessation"?
> [Question:] Then, what is this "analytical cessation"?
> [Answer:] The root [text] says, "That which is a separation."
> [Question:] Then what is a "separation"? This explanation, which is circular with the [other] explanation—an "analytical cessation"—does not have the capacity to shed light on what [a cessation's] nature is. (8b) Therefore, you have to express its nature in another way.
> [Answer:] Its nature is an object of individual knowledge only by Superiors. It can only be said that there exists a distinct substance that is permanent and virtuous called a "separation" and an "analytical cessation."[204]

Jamyang Shayba's textbook on Vasubandhu's *Treasury of Higher Knowledge* says:

> Vaibhāṣikas assert that the entity of an analytical cessation is a substantially existent, permanent, and virtuous, unconditioned thing. For they assert it as unconditioned in the sense of lacking causes and conditions, a thing (*bhāva*) in that it performs the function of causing an affliction to cease, a permanent phenomenon in that it is non-disintegrating, an ultimate virtue, and substantially existent since its entity exists as separately identifiable.[205]

It is established [that the Sautrāntikas assert the three unconditioned phenomena to be neither substantially existent nor substantially established] because the Sautrāntikas assert that the unconditioned phenomena exist imputedly. This is because they assert that the three unconditioned phenomena are only imputedly existent and are only non-affirming negatives (*prasajya-pratiṣedha*). For they posit: 1) a mere absence of obstructive contact as space; 2) a mere separation from any kind of seed of an affliction through the wisdom of individual [that is, point by point, or successive] investigation as an analytical cessation; and 3) a mere lack of the production of something due to its conditions' being incomplete, rather than due to an individual analysis, as a non-analytical cessation; and thus they assert that these are neither substantially established nor substantially existent. Vasubandhu's *Explanation* says:

> The Sautrāntikas: Unconditioned things do not substantially exist because they do not exist as separate substances, like form, feeling, and so on. Then what are they? The mere nonexistence of an object of touch is space. Thus, in the dark, when no obstruction is found, such is apprehended as "space." The subtle increasers [that is, afflictions] and births that had been produced having stopped, the non-production of another [affliction] through the power of an individual analysis is an analytical cessation. The non-production that is due to the incompleteness of conditions, rather than due to an individual analysis, is a non-analytical cessation. For example, that which would have remained in the intermediate state, of concordant type with one who has died [but did not in fact do so because the person was reborn into another state].[206]

Furthermore, Jetāri's *Differentiation of the Texts of the Sugata (Sugatagrantamata-vibhaṅga Kārikā)* says:

> Space is like the son of a barren woman,
> Also, the two cessations are like space . . .[207]

And his own *Commentary (Sugatagrantamata-vibhaṅga Bhāṣya)* says:

> Space is similar to the son of a barren woman with regard to [a certain sort of] nonexistence. The two cessations resemble such space and they should be drawn out [in a similar way as is done here with space] . . .[208]

There are many debates about these which may be known through looking in the second chapter of Vasubandhu's *Explanation* and Jetāri's own commentary on his *Differentiation of the Texts of the Sugata*, and so on.

It is established [that the Vaibhāṣikas and the Sautrāntikas differ on whether or not to assert the aggregates to be substantially existent] because the Vaibhāṣikas assert the aggregates to be substantially existent and the Sautrāntikas assert them to be imputedly existent. The reason—[that the Vaibhāṣikas assert the aggregates to be substantially existent and the Sautrāntikas assert them to be imputedly existent]—follows because: 1) the Vaibhāṣikas assert that "form" (*rūpa*) and "form aggregate" (*rūpa-skandha*) are co-extensive, treating "form aggregate" (*rūpa-skandha*) as a descriptive determinative (*karmadhāraya*) compound since a form is itself an aggregate, and similarly, they assert that "feeling" and "feeling aggregate," and so on, are also co-extensive and that each of the five aggregates—form and so on—exists substantially; 2) the Sautrāntikas assert that whatever is a form is not necessarily a form aggregate, taking [*rūpa-skandha*] as "aggregate of forms," a dependent determinative (*tatpuruṣa*) compound, and they assert the four—feelings and so on—in a similar way and assert that each of the five aggregates exists imputedly.

The reason follows because although both the Vaibhāṣikas and the Sautrāntikas agree in taking *skandha* to mean "a pile," in accordance with the statement [in Vasubandhu's *Treasury of Higher Knowledge*,] which says, "[*Skandha* means] 'pile,' [*āyatana* means] 'door of production,' and [*dhātu* means] 'type,'" they disagree in asserting whether [a *skandha*] exists substantially or imputedly, as is set forth at length in Vasubandhu's *Explanation* and in Rājaputra-Yaśomitra's *Commentary*.[209]

It is established [that they agree that *skandha* means "a pile"] because from among the three etymologies of *skandha* in Maitreya's *Differentiation of the Middle Way and the Extremes (Madhyānta Vibhaṅga)*, which says, "[*Skandha*] means 'manifold,' 'gathered together,' and 'thoroughly divided,'" and the four etymologies in Vasubandhu's *Reasonings for*

Explanations (Vyākhyāyukti), which says, "*Skandha* refers to 'pile,' 'shoulder,' 'trunk,' and 'part,'" and so forth, both of the Proponents of [Truly Existent External] Objects assert that *skandha* has the meaning of "pile."[210] Also, some sects, as well as the Cittamātrins and so on, assert that (9b) since *skandha* is also used to [mean] "shoulder," it means "carrying a burden," and they also assert that it has the meaning of "splitting up" or "categorizing as" form and so on. Also, there are many explanations in which the aggregates are treated within the framework of cyclic existence, such as the statement in Candrakīrti's *Supplement*, "The aggregates have suffering as their specific character."[211] I will not elaborate on the sources here.

It is established [that the Vaibhāṣikas and the Sautrāntikas disagree on whether to assert that an aggregate is substantially existent or imputedly existent] because the Sautrāntikas assert that, "Aggregates are imputedly existent, for 'aggregate' (*skandha*) means 'pile.' This is because a pile has the nature of being an aggregation of many substances. As examples, piled grain is called a *skandha* of grain, and the aggregation of the aggregates (*skandha*) of form and so on is only designated as the person, [although the person] does not substantially exist." To explain this assertion, Vasubandhu's *Explanation* says:

> Since *skandha* means "pile," the aggregates (*skandha*) are imputed existents because they are aggregations of many substances, as is a pile [of grain] and as is a person.[212]

As to this, the Vaibhāṣikas maintain, "It is not so, because even a single minute particle (*paramāṇu*) of a substance is a *skandha*." Vasubandhu's *Explanation* says, "It is not so, because even a single minute particle of a substance is a *skandha*."[213]

The Sautrāntikas: "So, instead of saying that *skandha* means 'pile,' you must give another meaning, because the meaning of 'pile' is not satisfied with regard to a single minute particle." Vasubandhu's *Explanation* says, "In that case, since there is no pile in a single [minute particle], it should not be said that *skandha* means 'pile.'"[214]

As to that, others, such as the Cittamātrins, maintain, "Even minute particles are *skandha* because the meaning of *skandha* need not be posited only as 'pile,' but [also] as having the meanings of 'that which carries the burden of an action' and 'category.' For example, sin is purified (10a) through obeisance, confessing one's sins and so on; virtue is accumulated through admiring [one's own and others' virtues] and so on; and virtue is increased through dedication [of one's merit]; and these three [practices] are called *skandha*." Vasubandhu's *Explanation* says:

> Others say that *skandha* has the meaning of "that which carries the burden of an activity" or "category." This is like a speaker's saying, "The three *skandha* that I will offer are to be offered purely."[215]

Pūrṇavardhana explains that here, the "burden of an activity" refers to the effects of the aggregates and "carrying" refers to the dependence of these effects upon the aggregates. Also, as to what is the burden and what is the burdened, the six sources (*āyatana*) are the burden of the five aggregates, attachment is the burden of feeling, and so on, [according to the formulation of dependent-arising]. As to that, the Sautrāntikas say: "Since those assertions contradict *sūtra*, they are incorrect; for *sūtra* says that *skandha* means only 'pile': 'All forms whatsoever—past, future, present, internal, external, coarse, subtle, bad, wonderful, distant, and nearby—all of those, lumped together as one, are counted as 'the aggregate of form.'"

Others, such as the Vaibhāṣikas, say: "In that sūtra, the eleven forms, as individuals, are indicated to be aggregates. Just as, for example, extensive statements [in *sūtra*] such as, 'What is an earth-constituent (*pṛthivī-dhātu*)? Hair on the head, body hair . . .,' teach that hairs and so on, as individuals, are earth-constituents, so also the earlier sūtra teaches that each form, for example, a past [form], individually is an aggregate." To explain this, Vasubandhu's *Explanation* says:

> There, past forms and so on, as individuals, are to be known as aggregates, because every one of these, past forms and so on, is a form aggregate.[216]

Sautrāntikas: "It is improper to understand (10b) the sūtra's meaning in that way; otherwise, [Buddha] would not have said, 'all those, lumped together as one,' but, 'all of them are aggregates,' but such was not said." To explain this, Vasubandhu's *Explanation* says:

> It cannot be understood in that way, for it says, "all those, lumped together as one." Therefore, the aggregates of form are imputed existents, as is a pile.[217]

Rājaputra-Yaśomitra explains this as the master Vasubandhu's own system.

Vaibhāṣikas: "Thus, it [absurdly] follows that each of the ten sources that have form exist imputedly because the composite of many minute particles of the eye sense faculty is posited as an eye-source [that is, eye sense faculty, which is a source of the eye consciousness], and the composite of many minute particles of color is posited as a visible form-source (*rūpāyatana*), and it is similarly the case [with all the sources] through to [and including the] body-source and the tangible-object-source. This is because the five sense consciousnesses depend upon composites [of particles] and observe composites [of particles]." To explain this, Vasubandhu's *Explanation* says:

> Therefore, [absurdly,] even sources that possess form would exist [only] imputedly because many minute particles of the eye [sense faculty] and so on serve as the door for producing [a consciousness].[218]

To this, the Sautrāntikas say: "Not just a composite of many particles is posited as an eye-source, form-source, and so on. For each minute particle of the eye sense faculty is an eye-source, each minute particle of color is a form-source, and this is similarly the case with all the sources through to [and including] the body-source and the tangible-object-source. You say that just aggregations could be sources and the individual [minute particles themselves] could not be posited as sources since minute particles become doors for producing sense consciousnesses through being dependent on one another. But if this were the case, since even the sense faculties and their objects become doors for generating a sense consciousness through being dependent on one another, then these could not individually be sources [either]. But such is not the case. For even you assert that (11a) the sūtras speak of the 'twelve sources.' [So you Vaibhāṣikas cannot convict us Sautrāntikas of an inconsistency in our maintaining that the aggregates imputedly exist whereas the sources substantially exist.] Also, as the *Detailed Explanation (Vibhāṣā)* says:

> If the aggregates are asserted to be imputedly existent, a minute particle must be asserted to be one [part] of any of the ten physical constituents, and to be one [part] of any of the ten physical sources, and to be a part of a form aggregate [and cannot itself be either a constituent, a source, or an aggregate]. If the aggregates are not asserted to be imputedly existent [but substantially existent], a minute particle must be asserted to be a constituent, or a source, or a form aggregate.

"Also, although minute particles are [only] a single class of form aggregate, one imputes [to it] the convention, 'form aggregate,' as when in the world one says that a cloth burned when just one part of it did so." [That is, the fact that single particles are called "form aggregates" does not entail that the class of "form aggregate" is exhausted in single particles.] To explain this, Vasubandhu's *Explanation* says:

> This is not the case [that is, it is not the case that our Sautrāntika position that the aggregates exist only imputedly by reason of being composites of particles entails that even the sources would exist only imputedly], for each [particle] in the collections [that are sources] is a causal entity. Or, since [sense] objects [serve as] cooperative [conditions] (*sahābhu-hetu*), the sense faculties [which empower the sense consciousnesses to apprehend their objects] would [absurdly] not be sources separate from them. The *Detailed Explanation* says, "Since an Abhidharmika views the aggregates as imputed existents, he propounds that a minute particle is a section of one of the constituents, one of the sources, or one of the aggregates. However, when one does not view [the aggregates as imputedly existent], one propounds that a minute particle is a single

> constituent, a single source, or a single aggregate." Although it is [just] one section [within the larger class], it is designated [with the name of the] whole. It is similar, for example, to saying, "the cloth burned," when referring to a partially burned cloth.[219]

The third root reason—[that the Vaibhāṣikas and the Sautrāntikas differ on whether or not shape substantially exists]—is established because, while the Vaibhāṣikas assert that shape substantially exists, the Sautrāntikas assert that shape imputedly exists. The reason follows because the Vaibhāṣikas assert that there are four possibilities between that which exists as a shape and that which exists as a color [that is, that there are things in each of the following categories: 1) both shape and color, 2) neither shape nor color, 3) shape but not color, and 4) color but not shape. Specifically,] that which exists as a shape and does not exist as a color is asserted to be the longness and so forth that are perceivable by the body. Therefore, they assert that independently of its seeing color, the eye consciousness can apprehend the longness and so forth (11b) that are perceivable by the body.

[*Note*: This argument is based on the fact that the Vaibhāṣikas considered "shape" to be a visible-form-source (*rūpāyatana*), and therefore, to be substantially existent. A visible-form-source must be an object of the eye consciousness. And the Buddha is quoted here as saying that a visible-form-source can be perceived only by the eye consciousness. Both the Vaibhāṣikas and the Sautrāntikas accept the Buddha's statement as authoritative, but it apparently caused a problem for the Vaibhāṣikas because shapes are sometimes felt without being seen (as in the dark), which points to the fact that shapes are known through the sense of touch as well as through sight. This created no problem for the Sautrāntikas who considered shape to be something merely imputed by the mind to particular configurations of particles. But it put the Vaibhāṣikas in the difficult position of trying to explain how we come to know shape merely by touching something if shape was substantially existent and something separate, therefore, from the object of touch. For if one was to accept the Buddha's statement, a visible-form-source (here, supposedly, the shape) could not be directly apprehended by the body consciousness (that is, through touch), but only by the eye consciousness.

The Vaibhāṣikas answered this problem by saying that shape is not actually the object of the body consciousness itself. The body consciousness, unlike the eye consciousness (which can directly apprehend shape), is "blind" to the direct apprehension of the shape. But the reason we can feel something in the dark and know its substantially existent shape is that its shape makes itself known to us through inference. Neither the eye consciousness nor the body consciousness is in direct contact with it, but since a shape always accompanies an object of touch (everything we can physically touch has a shape), the object of touch calls forth an invariable and therefore definite knowledge of the accompanying shape.

The Sautrāntikas responded to this by pointing out that although an object of touch always has, or is "accompanied by" shape, this is true only insofar as there is always *some* shape, but the problem is to explain how specific shapes are not invariably tied to specific objets of touch.]

Concerning this, the Sautrāntikas assert: "Shape does not substantially exist because the conventions, longness and so on, are designated to different types of arrangements of particles of color. For example, depending upon the different ways in which a torch is moved, it appears to be long, or circular and so on. If the shape existed as a different substantial entity from the color and the tangible object, it would [absurdly] follow that it would be an object of apprehension by two sense consciousnesses, because when it is seen by an eye consciousness, it is known to be long and so on; and also, when it is touched by the body consciousness, it is known to be long and so on. Moreover, just as different arrangements of the tangible object particles are apprehended as long and so on, so also one should believe colors to be like that." Vasubandhu's *Explanation* says:

> According to the Sautrāntikas, "Shape does not substantially exist . . . Where a lot of color has arisen in a single direction, one imputes it to be a 'long form'; one imputes what has fewer [color particles] in relation to that to be 'short'; one imputes what has many [particles] in four directions to be a 'rectangle'; if they are equal in all [directions], one imputes it to be

> 'round.' All [shapes] are similar. For example, when one perceives a torch being continuously moved quickly from one place to another, it is 'long,' but when one perceives it [moved] in all [directions], one thinks that it is 'round.' However, [these] shapes are not separate substances [that is, forms]. If [the shape] were [a separate substance from the color and the tangible object, that is, if it were a form], "[The form] would be apprehended by two [sense faculties]," for seeing it with the eye, one understands 'long,' and feeling it with the body sense faculty, one understands ['long']. Thus, [shape] would be apprehended by two sense faculties. However, [Buddha] said, 'Two [sense consciousnesses] do not apprehend visible-form-sources, [only the eye sense consciousness does].' Tangible objects are apprehended as 'long' and so on, just as you believe it to be with regard to color."[220]

The Vaibhāṣikas: "When something is felt by the body consciousness, the knowledge of it as long and so on is not a direct apprehension of longness and so on by the body consciousness but an inference of the shape (12a) [made] by the force of directly knowing the other [that is, the actual object of the body consciousness]. For example, seeing the color of a fire, we infer heat, and smelling the odor of a flower, we infer its color." To explain this, Vasubandhu's *Explanation* says:

> As for that, since [the shape] abides together with the tangible object, knowledge of the shape at that time is just [an association in] one's memory, not a direct apprehension. For example, from seeing the form of a fire, there arises the memory of heat, and from smelling the odor of a flower, there arises the memory of color.[221]

About this, the master [Vasubandhu] and the Sautrāntikas say: "Because wherever the color of fire exists, heat must definitely exist and wherever the smell of a magnolia flower exists, color must definitely exist, it is reasonable to infer them. However, because wherever the tangible object softness exists, a long shape does not definitely exist, it is unreasonable to infer [the presence of a certain] shape from [the presence of a certain] tangible object.

"If it were the case that shapes such as longness could be inferred from tangible objects such as softness even though those two need not abide together, it would [absurdly] follow that one could also infer colors, such as yellow, from tangible objects, such as softness. Or in another way, it would [absurdly] follow that just as colors, such as yellow, are not known through the direct knowledge by the body consciousness of tangible objects such as softness, it would not be possible to know shapes, such as longness either. But this is not the case. Therefore, longness and so on are imputed to the arrangements of tangible object particles." To explain that assertion, Vasubandhu's *Explanation* says:

> Because of an invisible [concomitance], the bringing to mind of one thing due to [the presence of] another is reasonable. However, the tangible object due to which this [shape] is brought to mind (12b) is not in the least definitely [concomitant] with any [particular] shape. However, if, despite there being no definite concomitance [of tangible objects with certain shapes], shape could definitely be brought to mind, then the color could be as well. Or in another way, just as the color [is not in fact brought to mind through bringing to mind the tangible object], so [absurdly] the shape could not be ascertained. However, that is not the case. Therefore, it is unreasonable [to assert] that a shape is brought to mind due to [the presence of a] tangible object.[222]

The Sautrāntikas: "When one views an arrangement [of particles] as a long shape, [it being built] from the aggregation of a variety of shapes such as long, short, round, and square, aside from its being seen as a long shape, it does not appear as a variety of shapes, such as round and square. Therefore, [if shape substantially existed], those various shapes would have to be transformed into a single long [shape], but that is unreasonable. It is similar to the fact that a variegated [collection] of colors, such as white, red, blue, and yellow, is not transformed into a single yellow [color]. If shapes, such as long and so on, existed substantially, as do colors such as yellow, etc., then just as the various colors, such as yellow, exist as minute particles, so various particles of shape, such as long [shape particles], would necessarily exist, but they do not. This is because if longness, shortness, and so on did exist in that way, they would not be directionally partless." To explain the Sautrāntikas' assertion, Vasubandhu's *Explanation* says:

> Since an unrolled painting does not appear as [a confused variety of] shapes [but is viewed as a particular and coherent whole], the many [shapes] would [absurdly] have to become a single kind [of shape]. However, that is unreasonable, and so it is with colors. Therefore, shapes do not substantially exist. Shapes that existed [in their own substantial entities] as obstructive forms would, without question, exist as minute particles; there, many [particles] abiding in a [particular] way are just imputed to be long and so on. If, nevertheless, you assert that we impute as long and so on, just "minute particles of shape" abiding as such, then since they are not established [as such], this is just [unreasonably] holding onto your [former] position, [which we have already refuted]. If their specific characteristics were established (13a), a composite of them would be possible. However, since the shape components are not established by way of their own entities, as are colors and so on, how could there exist a composite of them?[223]

This says that minute particles of shape do not exist, but does not say that minute particles do not have shape. For, it is said in Jamyang Shayba's textbook that the shape of a minute particle is spherical. Nevertheless, this must be examined, since Tsongkhapa's *Golden Rosary* says, "The [texts on] higher knowledge (*abhidharma*) explain that minute particles do not have shape."[224]

Third Debate

Someone says: It follows that in this context [of the Vaibhāṣikas and the Sautrāntikas Following Scripture], whatever is an ultimate truth is necessarily without parts, because Chim Jamyang's *Commentary on (Vasubandhu's) "Treasury of Higher Knowledge"* says, "It is asserted to exist conventionally because of having parts, and the *Ornament for (Dharmakīrti's) Seven Treatises* says:

> This explanation in Vasubandhu's *Treasury of Higher Knowledge* is the system of the Sautrāntikas who assert that whatever is substantially established must be without parts.[225]

Our Reply: [These passages] do not entail [that in these tenet systems whatever is an ultimate truth is necessarily without parts], for [these statements were made] in consideration [of the fact] that these systems' way of positing something to ultimately exist derives from its not having parts in the end.

[That whatever is an ultimate truth is necessarily without parts] cannot be accepted, for both the Vaibhāṣikas and the Sautrāntikas Following Scripture assert that each of the ten physical sources—colors, such as blue, and the eye, and so forth—exist substantially and are ultimate truths [even though they have parts]. The reason follows because these [sources] are clearly described in Yaśomitra's *Commentary on (Vasubandhu's) "Explanation"* to be asserted as substantially existent. Also, there is no Śrāvaka school that asserts that if something substantially exists, it is not necessarily an ultimate truth.

[*Note*: Ngawang Belden's argument is that some of the things included as physical sources (*gzhugs can gyi skye mched*), and therefore as ultimate truths, have parts. A patch of blue, for example, is a physical source, but it is a mass of smaller patches of blue, which are also physical sources. But no matter how much one cuts up a patch of blue, the result is always patches of blue. Thus, even though the patch of blue has parts, it fulfills the *Abhidharmakośa's* carefully worded definition of an ultimate truth, because the parts, being uniform with the whole, receive the same name as the whole. That something does not have parts "in the end" apparently means that no matter how much it is cut up, nothing different from what one started with will be encountered. Thus, something that has parts can be strictly "partless" because, as is made clear in the fourth debate, if the parts "are" the whole (that is, a blue part *is* just blue), the whole is "partless."]

Fourth Debate

Someone says: It follows that [in these systems] whatever is without parts is necessarily either form or consciousness, because they do not assert anything to be without parts other than directionally partless particles and partless moments of consciousness.

Our reply: It is not established [that they do not assert anything to be without parts other than directionally partless particles and partless moments of consciousness] because in these systems, the three unconditioned phenomena are also without parts. The reason follows because Śāntarakṣita's *Ornament for the Middle Way (Madhyamakālaṃkāra)* is proving to [some of] our own [Buddhist] sectarians that the three unconditioned phenomena have parts, where it says:

> Also, to the system propounding that the unconditioned
> are objects of knowledge (13b)
> Of a mind arisen from meditation,
> [I say that] they are not one,
> [that is, as you assert, without parts,]
> Because they are consecutively related to consciousness.[226]

For Śāntarakṣita's own commentary (*Madhyamakālaṃkāravṛtti*) says:

> Someone [that is, a Vaibhāṣika,] says: "There is no contradiction in their having a nature of oneness, in accordance with the system of those of us among our own schools [that is, the Vaibhāṣikas] who propound that, 'The unconditioned that is the object of observation of a consciousness that arises merely by the power of meditation, and which does not accord with any of the operations of conditioned things, and which does not even require the existence of an observer of it, is the object of a consciousness of suchness; therefore, it exists ultimately.'"[227]

Moreover, it follows that [for the Vaibhāṣikas] the three unconditioned phenomena are partless because of their not having directional parts, such as eastern or western parts, that are of their entities and that are not [the unconditioned phenomena] themselves, and not having former and later temporal parts that are of their entities and that are not [the unconditioned phenomena] themselves. This proves that the three unconditioned phenomena are partless because this is the meaning of being partless. For the *Ornament for (Dharmakīrti's) Seven Treatises* says:

> Therefore, that something does not possess many different substantial entities that are eastern or western parts that are of its entity and that are not it means that it is partless. In general, that something is "empty of east and west" does not mean that it is partless. A minute particle is a different substantial entity from the minute particle to the east of it, but [the latter] is not a part of it [and thus not of its entity]; therefore, although [something] east of it exists, it does not come to have directional parts. Similarly, with respect to a shortest moment of time, that it is lacking earlier and later [portions] that are of its entity means that it is temporally partless. In general, something does not come to have temporal parts due to there being former or later [periods of time] with respect to it.[228]

Fifth Debate

Someone says: It follows that the three unconditioned things are emptinesses because they are ultimate truths.

Our reply: It does not follow at all [that in this system, whatever is an ultimate truth is an emptiness], but it is established that the three unconditioned things are ultimate truths because they exist ultimately. This is established by the passage that was cited just above from Śāntarakṣita's own commentary.

It cannot be accepted that [the three unconditioned things are emptinesses] because, in this system (14a), "emptiness" refers to the emptiness and selflessness from among the sixteen [attributes of the four noble truths]: impermanence, and so on. This is because the meaning of Vasubandhu's root text and commentary is established [where the root text] says, "Emptiness refers to selflessness and emptiness," and so on.[229]

Sixth Debate

Someone says: It follows that the Śrāvaka schools do not assert emptiness because they assert that it is not necessary to realize emptiness in order to achieve liberation. The reason follows because there exists a way of debating [used by the Śrāvakas as reported in] Śāntideva's *Engaging in the Bodhisattva Deeds (Bodhisattvacaryāvatāra)*, etc., which states:

> One is liberated through seeing the truths;
> What is the use of seeing emptiness?[230]

Also Gyaltsap's *Commentary* says:

> Some Śrāvaka sectarians [assert] not only that it is not necessary to realize emptiness even in order to achieve Buddhahood, but also do not even assert the name "selflessness of phenomena."[231]

Our reply: These passages do not entail that the Śrāvaka schools do not assert emptiness because these mean that they do not assert, as an object of meditation, an emptiness which is not included in the sixteen attributes of the four [noble] truths as asserted by them. The reason follows because there are no aspects of the truths besides the sixteen—impermanence and so on—which are spoken of in the sūtras on higher knowledge (*abhidharma*) and although a suchness which is not included in these [sixteen] is explained in the scriptural collections of the Mahāyāna, [the Śrāvaka schools] assert it to be unreliable like the suchness taught by the Ākāśadevas.[232] Also, the Blessed One did not teach Śrāvaka sectarians an emptiness that is a lack of inherent existence, etc., as is set forth in the scriptural collections of the Mahāyāna.

It is established that [there are no aspects of the truths besides the sixteen—impermanence and so on—which are spoken of in the sūtras on higher knowledge] because Vasubandhu's *Treasury of Higher Knowledge* says, "There are no aspects other than the stainless sixteen."[233] It is established that [although a suchness which is not included in these sixteen attributes is explained in the scriptural collections of the Mahāyāna, the Śrāvaka schools assert it to be unreliable like the suchness taught by the Ākāśadevas] because Bhāvaviveka's *Heart of the Middle Way (Madhyamaka Hṛdaya)* [says], in giving the position of the Śrāvaka schools:

> [If] the truths seen are not suchness,
> It follows that suchness does not exist.
> We do not assert what is like that taught
> By the Ākāśadevas to be suchness.[234]

His own commentary says:

> [Śrāvaka sectarian:] Even in the Mahāyāna [the truths] are sufferings, origins, cessations, and paths, but it is renowned that [the Mahāyāna] has the teaching that one does not pass completely beyond sorrow by knowing sufferings, etc. [However,] if the truths that are seen are not suchness (14b), then say what other suchness there is which is not those.
> [Opponent, that is, Bhāvaviveka himself:] There is the suchness taught by the Mahāyāna.
> [Śrāvaka sectarian:] That is not reasonable because it, like that taught by the Ākāśadevas, is something other than the truths seen. [The Ākāśadevas] teach the following sort of suchness: They assert that if one kills an ant by piercing it with a golden needle in a golden vessel, it will be released from cyclic existence and the killer will accumulate the seed of liberation [from cyclic existence]. They say that, "Killing oxen, etc., and copulation serve as causes [of rebirth] in a high state, etc."[235]

It is established [that the Blessed One did not teach Śrāvaka sectarians an emptiness that is a lack of things' inherent existence as is set forth in the scriptural collections of the Mahāyāna] because Śrāvaka sectarians are not fit vessels for the teaching of the profound emptiness. This reason entails [that the Blessed One did not teach Śrāvaka sectarians an emptiness that is a lack of things' inherent existence as is set forth in the scriptural collections of the Mahāyāna] because many sūtras and treatises explain that the Buddha spoke doctrines in terms of [different kinds of] disciples. Nāgārjuna's *Treatise on the Middle Way* says:

> The Buddha taught that
> All are real, are not real,
> Are real and unreal,
> Are neither unreal nor real.[236]

For the purpose of initially instilling [disciples with respect for himself] with the thought, "He is omniscient, knowing without exception the ways in which the world arises," [the Buddha] says that all environments and beings, such as the aggregates, the constituents, and the sources, are real, or true. Then, when that respect has been instilled, he says that these conditioned things are unreal, that is, "impermanent," since they change into other things every moment.

Then, he says that all of these environments and beings are, relative to a childish person, real—that is, they [seem to] abide in their own entities for a second moment after their own [moment of] time, and that these are, relative to a Superior's wisdom attained subsequent to meditative equipoise, unreal in the sense that [a Superior sees that] they do not abide in their own entities for a second moment after their own [moment of] time.

Then, for those who are fit vessels for the generation of the profound view in their [mental] continuum, he says that the unreal, those which change into something else each moment, are not established through their own entities and that also the real, those which do not change into something else each moment, are not established through their own entities. (15a) Thus, it is said that the Buddha teaches doctrines in these four stages to suit the minds of disciples. Nāgārjuna's *Precious Garland (Ratnāvalī)* says:

> Just as grammarians have [their students]
> Read a model of the alphabet,

So the Buddha teaches his disciples
The doctrines they can bear.

To some he teaches doctrines
To turn them away from sins;
To some, doctrines to achieve merit;
To others, [doctrines] based on duality.

To some he teaches doctrines that are not dualistic.
To some he teaches what is profound and frightens
the fearful:
That which has an essence of emptiness and compassion,
The means of achieving enlightenment.[237]

yadeva's *Treatise in Four Hundred Stanzas* says:

He teaches "existence," "nonexistence," "existence and
nonexistence,"
And also "neither existence nor nonexistence."
According to the [disciple's] sickness,
Couldn't all [of these] be called "medicine"?[238]

:venth Debate

meone says: According to the Vaibhāṣikas, suchness is a conditioned ing, because if it were unconditioned, [then among] the objects of servation of an uncontaminated consciousness there would have to be unspecified unconditioned thing, whereas the root text and commen- y on Vasubandhu's *Treasury of Higher Knowledge* say that there is no ch thing, and there are no unconditioned phenomena that are not cluded in the three explained in Vasubandhu's *Treasury of Higher 1owledge.* For Rājaputra-Yaśomitra says:

The mention of three types limits it to just those. There are some, like the Vātsīputrīya School, who maintain that the unconditioned is exhausted in just the one—nirvāṇa. The

> Vaiśeṣikas speak of many unconditioned things, minute particles and so forth. [The unconditioned] are limited to just these in order to refute their systems.[239]

Our reply: It follows that it is incorrect [that suchness is a conditioned thing for the Vaibhāṣikas] because the emptiness and selflessness of true sufferings are not the objects of observation of a consciousness of sufferings. The reason follows because if they were the objects of observation of a consciousness of sufferings, it would follow that they would be the objects of observation of a consciousness of origins. The reason follows because, since it is said that the two, the consciousness of sufferings (15b) and that of origins, are differentiated by their [subjective] aspects and not by their objects of observation, the objects of observation of those two are mutually inclusive. There is also no consciousness of origins that observes emptiness and selflessness.

Moreover, [your position that suchness is a conditioned thing] is incorrect because the two—the objects of observation and objects of comprehension of an uncontaminated consciousness that realizes true sufferings as selfless—are mutually exclusive. The reason follows because the objects of observation of that [consciousness] are necessarily conditioned phenomena, [whereas] the objects of comprehension of that [consciousness] are necessarily unconditioned phenomena.

[*Note*: A consciousness of sufferings *observes* true sufferings (conditioned phenomena) but *comprehends* their selflessness or suchness (unconditioned phenomena). Thus, the object observed by such a consciousness and the object comprehended by it are, respectively, a conditioned phenomenon and an unconditioned phenomenon, and since these two objects of this consciousness are mutually exclusive, we know that in the Vaibhāṣika system the conditioned and the unconditioned are mutually exclusive, and thus, that suchness cannot be a conditioned phenomenon. This is Ngawang Belden's argument.]

It is established [that the objects of observation of that consciousness are necessarily conditioned phenomena] because they are necessarily true sufferings. That is because there is nothing uncontaminated (*anāsrava*) about them. If you say that this is not established, then it would follow that in the objects of observation of a consciousness of sufferings, there would be more than six from among the ten phenomena (*dharma*).[240]

The second reason [that there are no unconditioned phenomena that are not included in the three explained in Vasubandhu's *Treasury of Higher Knowledge*] is not established because whatever is an object of comprehension of that [consciousness of sufferings] is necessarily a subtle selflessness. It is easy to prove that [whatever is an object of comprehension of that] consciousness of sufferings is necessarily a subtle selflessness. It follows from this reason that [there are no unconditioned phenomena that are not included in the three explained in Vasubandhu's *Treasury of Higher Knowledge*] because there is a reason for [Vasubandhu's] not [explicitly] positing, [for example,] the liberation of wishlessness which realizes emptiness and selflessness [which is unconditioned]. Vasubandhu's *Explanation* says:

> Because of being similar to nirvāṇa, the mind (*manas*) does not arise by way of emptiness and selflessness.[241]

And Pūrṇavardhana says:

> Although truths that are sufferings are apprehended by means of the aspects of emptiness and selflessness, the arising of the mind is not with regard to that truth of suffering. Why? Because they [emptiness and selflessness] are similar to nirvāṇa. Emptiness and selflessness are characteristics even of nirvāṇa because of being the general characteristics of all phenomena.[242]

This proves [my point—that Vasubandhu has a reason for not positing emptiness and selflessness (suchness) as separate unconditioned things—] because according to you, one would have to assert the unconditioned emptiness and selflessness in the context of nirvāṇa and the emptiness and selflessness in the context of true sufferings as divisions of the unconditioned, but that is unreasonable.

[*Note*: Ngawang Belden's argument here is that Vasubandhu did not posit "suchness" (*tathatā*) as a fourth division of unconditioned things, as is done in the Mahāyāna, because, in order to protect himself in debate, he did not wish to isolate emptiness and selflessness, which are "suchnesses," apart from other phenomena. Yaśomitra's statement above, indicating that emptiness and selflessness are characteristics of all phenomena—both conditioned and unconditioned—gives Ngawang Belden his reason for arguing that Vasubandhu implicitly accepted emptiness and selflessness as unconditioned, that is, as "similar to nirvāṇa," even though he did not put them in a separate category of the unconditioned. For if—as Ngawang Belden's opponent argues—Vasubandhu did not accept emptiness and selflessness, even implicitly, as unconditioned, then since emptiness and selflessness apply both to conditioned and unconditioned phenomena (as characteristics of all phenomena), there would have to be a category of "conditioned emptiness and selflessness" as well as an unconditioned emptiness and selflessness, which is absurd. This is the fault that Vasubandhu and Yaśomitra have tried to avoid. Therefore, although they knew that emptiness and selflessness were in fact unconditioned, Vasubandhu and Yaśomitra did not wish to isolate emptiness and selflessness (that is, suchness) as a separate category within the divisions of existents because, being the general characteristics of all phenomena, they are, we would say, "distributed" over all the categories, or they are generically "above" all the categories.]

This is because otherwise, there would be no way to find fault even with the assertion that the subtle selflessness of a true path is a true path and that the subtle selflessness of a true cessation is a true cessation. [That is, if emptiness and selflessness were not held in some sense to be "separate" unconditioned things, they would not be any different from the things they qualify.]

Furthermore, it follows that [in our own system] there are unconditioned phenomena (16a) which are not included in the three unconditioned phenomena because, although in our own system there are unconditioned phenomena which are not included in the three unconditioned phenomena, this does not preclude [our] limiting [them to three in some expositions] since limiting [them] to three is done in order to eliminate wrong conceptions [and does not preclude more categories of unconditioned phenomena]. This is because it is similar to the fact that even though in the upper [that is, the Mahāyāna system of] higher knowledge (*abhidharma*) it is explained that there are eight unconditioned phenomena—in addition to the three unconditioned phenomena [asserted by the Śrāvaka schools, there are also] the three suchnesses, such as the virtuous suchness (*kusala-tathatā*), and so on, the unfluctuating cessation (*acala-nirodha*), and the cessation of feelings and discrimination (*vedanā-saṃjñā-nirodha*)—this does not preclude that there be unconditioned phenomena which are not included in those [eight].

Eighth Debate

Someone says: It follows that the explanation that each of the minute particles of the five sense faculties is an eye-source, and so on, and that each of the minute particles of the five objects is a form-source, and so on, is incorrect because the minute particles of the five objects—form and so on—are not individually conditions that are the objects of observation of the sense consciousnesses. That the reason is so follows because they do not individually appear to the sense consciousnesses. The reason follows because when any of them abides singly, it does not appear to a sense consciousness.

Our reply: The reason [that when any of them abides singly, it does not appear to a sense consciousness] does not entail [that individually they do not appear to the sense consciousnesses] because although, [for example,] when a minute particle of blue abides singly, it does not appear to an eye consciousness apprehending blue, each of the minute particles of blue which exist in a collection of minute particles of blue appears to that [eye consciousness]. This is similar to the fact that although, for example, from a distance, a single strand of hair of a horse's tail does not appear to an eye consciousness, this does not preclude that from a distance the horse's tail appears to an eye consciousness. The reason follows because, despite their differences about whether or not [objects] cast their likenesses [to the sense consciousnesses], the Vaibhāṣikas, Sautrāntikas, and the Sautrāntika-Svātantrika-Mādhyamikas agree in asserting that each of the minute particles of the five objects appears to a sense consciousness.

It is established [that the Vaibhāṣikas, Sautrāntikas, and the Sautrāntika-Svātantrika-Mādhyamikas agree in asserting that each of the minute particles of the five objects appears to a sense consciousness], for:

1) The Vaibhāṣikas assert that the object and the consciousness are different substantial entities—even though they are simultaneous—by reason of the fact that the object is actually apprehended nakedly without its likeness appearing to the sense consciousness. It is said [in Jetāri's *Differentiation of the Texts of the Sugata*]:

> Awarenesses produced by the sense faculties actually know composites of minute [particles] without their [likenesses] appearing.[243]

2) According to the Sautrāntikas, since the blue is the observed-object-condition that casts its likeness to the eye consciousness apprehending blue, the blue and the eye consciousness apprehending blue are established as consecutive and are different substantial entities. However, because an eye consciousness apprehending blue clearly perceives the likeness of blue that is the same substantial entity with that [blue], it is posited that the blue is clearly perceived. It is said:

> According to the position [that asserts] that consciousness
> [has] aspects [that is, likenesses],
> Those two [that is, subject and object,] are actually different;
> But because [that object] is similar to the image,
> It is suitable that, merely imputedly, the [object] be sensed.[244]

3) According to the Cittamātrins (16b), the likeness of blue that appears to an eye consciousness apprehending blue is an aspect that appears by the power of predispositions, and is not an aspect that is cast by the object. Furthermore, although there is disagreement between the True Aspectarian [Cittamātrins] and the False Aspectarian [Cittamātrins] as to whether or not the likeness is one substantial entity with the con-

sciousness, they agree in asserting that [at least] they are not *different* substantial entities.[245]

4) According to the Sautrāntikas and the Sautrāntika-Svātantrika-Mādhyamikas, the blue is not established as a mass that is a composite of external particles, separate from the likeness of blue. Yet, they assert that [the blue] exists in a way that is not expressible as the same as or as different from the likeness. Fearing that [citing] the sources and so forth would be too much, I will not elaborate [on this here].

It is established [that the Vaibhāṣikas, Sautrāntikas, and the Sautrāntika-Svātantrika-Mādhyamikas agree in asserting that each of the minute particles of the five objects appears to a sense consciousness], for Jetāri's *Differentiation of the Texts of the Sugata* says:

> Awarenesses produced by the sense faculties actually know
> Composites of minute [particles] without likenesses [of them] appearing.

His own commentary says:

> Individually, they are beyond [the capacity of perception by] the sense faculties; only those that exist together with others of the same type become the objects of the sense faculties' activity. It is not at all necessary that those that cannot be perceived individually cannot be perceived even when gathered together. For, at a distance, hairs and so forth that are spread out, are not seen, but a mass [of them] is observed.[246]

Tsongkhapa's *Essence of Good Explanations* says:

> On the occasion of the aggregation of forms, sounds, and so on, each minute particle functions as an observed-object-condition of a sense consciousness. Therefore, it is not the case that they do not appear to it.[247]

This is also explained in Tsongkhapa's *Great Exposition of the Stages of the Path to Enlightenment*. Thus, we must analyze whether or not the text is corrupt in Jamyang Shayba's *Commentary* on his [own] root text of *Tenets*, where it says:

> Aggregations of others [that is, of things that are dissimilar], such as an army, exist imputedly. Composites of particles of a similar kind exist substantially. Each one is also suited to be an observed-object-condition (*ālambana-pratyaya*).[248]

His comment on that is:

> The Śrāvakas [that is, the Vaibhāṣikas] assert that an isolated minute particle is not an object of a sense consciousness; also, since a composite of minute particles is a collection-generality (*gaṇa-sāmānya*), it does not substantially exist and thus is not a proper object of a sense consciousness. [From the Sautrāntika-Svātantrika-Mādhyamika viewpoint] this is not correct, for as with the Sautrāntikas, on the occasion of the compounding of forms, sounds, and so on, each of the minute particles that exist in a collection of them are observed-object-conditions of a sense consciousness and their not being so would not be correct. For that [position] would also be damaged by the explanation [in *sūtra*] that the five collections of consciousnesses observe composites.[249]

If the text is not corrupt, (17a) subtle distinctions must be made [in order to show how] it does not contradict such [texts] as Tsongkhapa's *Essence of Good Explanations* [which says that the Śrāvakas hold that each minute particle in a composite is the object of a sense consciousness]. Thus, those who are analytical should continue looking into this in detail.

Moreover, although there are many points of controversy about the specifically characterized (*sva-lakṣaṇa*) and the generally characterized (*sāmānya-lakṣaṇa*) in the systems of the Śrāvaka schools which are very relevant here, fearing a great burden of words, I will not write [about it here]. Those can be known from the root texts and commentaries such as the two commentarial explanations of Vasubandhu's *Treasury of Higher Knowledge* [by Rājaputra-Yaśomitra and Pūrṇavardhana], and the sūtra on valid cognition [that is, Dignāga's *Compendium (of Teachings) on Valid Cognition (Pramāṇa-samuccaya)*], where it says:

> Because many objects generate them, they possess
> The specifically and generally characterized as the objects
> of their activity.[250]

And the third chapter, on "inference for oneself," in Dharmakīrti's *Commentary on (Dignāga's) "Compendium (of Teachings) on Valid Cognition,"* where it says:

> The compounded are collections.
> Those generalities have minds that are empowered toward
> them.
> An awareness of a generality is unquestionably
> Related to conceptual thought.[251]

Also, one should examine such questions as whether or not the minute particles of the five objects—forms and so on—are objects of comprehension by a sense consciousness, and whether or not, in this context [that is, tenet system], the five forms that are sources of phenomena (*dharmāyatana*) are asserted in accordance with those [forms] stated in *sūtra* and in Asaṅga's *Compendium of Higher Knowledge (Abhidharma-samuccaya)*, and whether or not the reference in Jamyang Shayba's textbook on Vasubandhu's *Treasury of Higher Knowledge* to the longness and so on that are objects of touch by the body consciousness, is the system of the Vaibhāṣikas. However, it is not possible to complete [such an examination] in a few words, so I will leave it for the time being.

Acknowledgments

I wish to thank the following people for their teaching, advice, counsel, and assistance to me: Jeffrey Hopkins, Harvey Aronson, Paul Groner, Geshe Belden Drakpa, Geshe Tenpa Gyaltsen, Geshe Yeshe Tupten, Don Lopez, Steven Rhodes, and my wife Belinda.

Abbreviations

The following abbreviations have been used in the Notes and Bibliography:

LVP Louis de La Vallée Poussin. *L'Abhidharmakośa de Vasubandhu.*

P Peking edition of the Tibetan Tripitaka, ed. Suzuki et al.

Toh Hakuju Ui, et al., eds. *A Complete Catalogue of the Tibetan Buddhist Canons* [*Chibetto Daizōkyō sōmokuroku*].

Bibliography

Agya Yongdzin (A-kya Yong-'dzin). *Gzhi'i sku gsum gyi rnam gshag rab gsal sgron me.* In *The Collected Works of A-kya Yong-dzin.* Vol. 1. New Delhi: Lama Guru Deva, 1971.

Amarasimha. *Amarakośa, with the Commentary of Maheśvara.* Ed. Chintamani Shastri Thatte and Franz Kielhorn. Bombay: Government Central Book Depot, 1877.

Andersen, Dines, and Helmer Smith, eds. *Suttanipāta.* London: Pali Text Society, 1913.

Āryadeva. *Catuḥśatakaśāstra.* P5246, vol. 95.

Asaṅga. *Abhidharmasamuccaya.* P5550, vol. 112. Also see Pradhan and Rahula.

Atīśa. *Satyadvayāvatāra.* P5298, vol. 101; P5380, vol. 103.

Bagchi, Prabodh Chandra. "Fundamental Problems of the Origins of Buddhism." *France-Asie/Asia* 17, no. 168 (July-August 1961): 2225-2241.

Bareau, André. "Trois traités sur les sectes bouddhiques attribués à Vasumitra, Bhavya et Vinītadeva." Part 1, *Journal Asiatique* 242 (1954): 229-266 [includes "Le cycle de la formation des schismes (*Samayabhedoparacanacakra*) de Vasumitra" (234-266)]; Part 2, *Journal Asiatique* 244 (1956): 167-200 [includes "L'explication des divisions entres les sectes (*Nikāyabhedavibhaṅga-vyākhyāna*) de Bhavya" (167-191) and "Le compendium descriptif des divisions des sectes dans le cycle de la formation des schismes (*Samayabhedoparacanacadrenikāyabhedopadarśana-saṃgraha*) de Vinītadeva" (192-200)].

———. *Les sectes bouddhiques du Petit Véhicule.* Saigon: École française d'Extrême-Orient, 1955.

Barua, Atasi, ed. *Petakopadesa.* London: Pali Text Society, 1949.

Basham, Arthur L. *History and Doctrines of the Ājīvikas, A Vanished Indian Religion.* London: Luzac, 1951.

Bechert, Heinz, ed. *Die Sprache der ältesten buddhistischen Überlieferung = The Language of the Earliest Buddhist Tradition.* Göttingen: Vandenhoeck und Ruprecht, 1980.

Bhartṛhari. *Vākyapadīya.* See Iyer.

Bhattacharya, Bishnupada. *Yāska's Nirukta and the Science of Etymology.* Calcutta: Firma K. L. Mukhopadhyay, 1958.

Bhāvaviveka. *Madhyamakahṛdaya.* P5255, vol. 96.

Biardeau, Madeleine. *Théorie de la connaissance et philosophie de la parole dans le brahmanisme classique.* Paris: Mouton, 1964.

Bloch, Jules. *Indo-Aryan: From the Vedas to the Modern Times.* Paris: Adrien-Maisonneuve, 1965.

———. *Les Inscriptions d'Aśoka.* Paris: Centre national de la recherche scientifique, 1950.

Bond, George Doherty. "The Problem of Interpretation in Theravāda Buddhism and Christianity." Ph.D. dissertation, Northwestern University, 1972.

Brough, John. *The Gāndhārī Dharmapada.* London: Oxford University Press, 1962.

Buddhadatta Thero, ed. *Sammoha-vinodanī Abhidhamma-piṭake Vibhaṅga-aṭṭhakathā.* London: Pali Text Society, 1923.

Buddhaghosa. *Aṭṭhasālinī* (*Dhammasaṅganī* commentary). See Müller and Tin.

———. *Manorathapūranī* (*Aṅguttara-nikāya* commentary). See Walleser.

———. *Sammohavinodanī* (*Vibhaṅga* commentary). See Buddhadatta Thero.

———. *Visuddhimagga.* See Ñāṇamoli.

Bu-dön (Bu-ston). *History of Buddhism.* See Obermiller.

Burrow, Thomas. *The Sanskrit Language.* London: Faber and Faber, 1966.

Candrakīrti. *Madhyamakāvatāra.* P5261, vol. 98. Also see La Vallée Poussin.

———. *Mūlamadhyamakavṛtti-prasannapadā.* P5260, vol. 98. Also see La Vallée Poussin.

Chakravarti, Prabhat Chandra. *Linguistic Speculations of the Hindus.* Calcutta: University of Calcutta, 1933.

———. *The Philosophy of Sanskrit Grammar.* Calcutta: University of Calcutta, 1930.

Chalmers, Lord Robert, ed. and trans. *Buddha's Teachings (Sutta-Nipāta).* Cambridge: Harvard University Press, 1931.

Chandra, Lokesh. *Eminent Tibetan Polymaths of Mongolia.* Śata-piṭaka Series, vol. 16. New Delhi: International Academy of Indian Culture, 1961.

———. *Materials for a History of Tibetan Literature.* Śata-piṭaka Series, vol. 29. New Delhi: International Academy of Indian Culture, 1963.

———. "Tibetan Works Printed by the Shöparkhang of the Potala." In *Jñanamuktāvalī*, ed. Claus Vogel, pp. 120-132. Lahore: International Academy of Indian Culture, 1959.

Chattopadhyaya, Alaka. *Atīśa and Tibet.* Calcutta: Indian Studies Past and Present, 1967.

Chavannes, Edouard. *Cinq cent contes et apologues: extraits du tripiṭaka chinois.* Paris: Ernest Leroux, 1911.

Chimpa, Lama, and Alaka Chattopadhyaya, trans. *Tāranātha's History of Buddhism in India.* Simla: Indian Institute of Advanced Study, 1970.

Conze, Edward, ed. *Buddhist Texts through the Ages.* New York: Harper and Row, 1964.

Conze, Edward, trans. *The Large Sutra on Perfect Wisdom.* Berkeley: University of California Press, 1975.

Coomaraswamy, Ananda K. "Some Pāli Words." *Harvard Journal of Asiatic Studies* 4 (1939): 116-190.

Cousins, L., et al., eds. *Buddhist Studies in Honour of I. B. Horner.* Dordrecht: D. Reidel, 1974.

Coward, Harold G., and K. Kunjunni Raja, eds. *The Philosophy of the Grammarians.* Princeton: Princeton University Press, 1990.

Cozort, Daniel. *Unique Tenets of the Middle Way Consequence School.* Ithaca, N. Y.: Snow Lion Publications, 1998.

Cozort, Daniel, and Craig Preston. *Buddhist Philosophy: Losang Gönchok's Short Commentary to Jamyang Shayba's* Root Text on Tenets. Ithaca, N. Y.: Snow Lion Publications, 2003.

Davidson, Ronald M. "An Introduction to the Standards of Scriptural Authenticity in Indian Buddhism." In *Chinese Buddhist Apocrypha,* ed. Robert E. Buswell, pp. 291-325. Honolulu: University of Hawai'i Press, 1990.

Demiéville, Paul. "L'origine des sectes bouddhiques d'apres Paramārtha." In his *Choix d'études bouddhiques,* pp. 113-172. Leiden: E. J. Brill, 1973.

Demiéville, Paul, ed. *Hōbōgirin: Dictionnaire encyclopedique du bouddhisme d'apres les sources chinoises et japonaises.* Tokyo: Maison Franco-Japonaise, 1929.

Demiéville, Paul, and Junjirō Takakusu, eds. *Hōbōgirin,* Supplementary Volume, *Tables du Taishō Issaikyō.* Tokyo: Maison Franco-Japonaise, 1931.

Deshpande, Madhav M., and Peter Edwin Hook, eds. *Aryan and Non-Aryan in India.* Ann Arbor: University of Michigan, 1979.

Devendrabuddhi. *Pramāṇavārttikapañjikā.* P5717(b), vol. 130.

Dharmakīrti. *Pramāṇavārttika.* P5709, vol. 130.

Dutt, Nalinaksha. *Aspects of Mahayana Buddhism and Its Relations to Hinayana.* London: Luzac, 1930.

———. *Buddhist Sects in India.* Calcutta: Firma K. L. Mukhopadhyay, 1970.

———. *Three Principal Schools of Buddhism.* Calcutta: C. O. Book Agency, 1939.

Dwivedi, R. C., ed. *Studies in Mīmāṃsā: Dr. Mandan Mishra Felicitation Volume.* Delhi: Motilal Banarsidass, 1994.

Edgerton, Franklin. *Buddhist Hybrid Sanskrit Grammar and Dictionary.* 2 vols. Repr., Delhi: Motilal Banarsidass, 1972.

Fausbøll, Viggo, ed. *The Jātaka: Together with Its Commentary.* Vol. 6. London: Trübner & Co., 1896.

Feer, Léon, ed. *The Saṃyutta-Nikāya of the Sutta-piṭaka.* 6 vols. London: Pali Text Society, 1884-1904.

First Dalai Lama (dGe-'dun-grub). *mDzod tik thar lam gsal byed / Dam pa'i chos mngon pa'i mdzod kyi rnam par bshad pa thar lam gsal byed.* In *The Collected Works of dGe-'dun-grub-pa.* Vol. 3. Gangtok: Dodrup Lama Sangye, 1979.

———. *Tshad ma rigs rgyan / Tshad ma'i bstan bcos chen po rigs pa'i rgyan.* In *The Collected Works of dGe-'dun-grub-pa.* Vol. 4. Gangtok: Dodrup Lama Sangye, 1979.

Foucaux, Philippe Édouard, trans. *La Lalita Vistara: Development des jeux.* Vol. 1. Annales du Musée Guimet, vol. 6. Paris: Ernest Leroux, 1884.

Frauwallner, Erich. *The Earliest Vinaya and the Beginnings of Buddhist Literature.* Rome: Is.M.E.O., 1956.

Gächter, Othmar. *Hermeneutics and Language in Pūrva Mīmāṃsā: A Study in Śābara Bhāṣya.* Delhi: Motilal Banarsidass, 1983.

Geiger, Wilhelm. *Pāli Literature and Language.* Trans. Balakrishna Ghosh. Repr., New Delhi: Oriental Books Reprint Corporation, 1978.

Gerow, Edwin. *A Glossary of Indian Figures of Speech.* The Hague: Mouton, 1971.

Gönchok Jigmay Wangbo (dKon-mchog-'jigs-med-dbang-po). *Grub pa'i mtha'i rnam par bzhag pa rin po che'i phreng ba.* Dharamsala: Shesrig Parkhang, 1969.

Guenther, Herbert. *Philosophy and Psychology in the Abhidharma.* Berkeley: Shambhala, 1976.

Hacker, Paul. *Vivarta: Studien zur Geschichte der illusionistischen Kosmologie und Erkenntnistheorie der Inder.* Mainz: Verlag der Wissenschaften und der Literatur, 1953.

Hardy, Edmund, ed. *The Netti-pakaraṇa, with Extracts from Dhammapāla's Commentary.* London: Pali Text Society, 1902.

Herzberger, Radhika. *Bhartṛhari and the Buddhists: An Essay in the Development of Fifth and Sixth Century Indian Thought.* Dordrecht: D. Reidel, 1986.

Hirakawa, Akira. *Index to the Abhidharmakośa.* Tokyo: Daizo Shuppan Kabushiki Kaisha, 1973.

———. "The Rise of Mahāyāna Buddhism and Its Relationship to the Worship of Stūpas." *Memoirs of the Research Department of the Tōyō Bunko* 22 (1963): 57-106.

Hofinger, Marcel. *Étude sur le concile de Vaiśālī.* Louvain: Bureau du Muséon, 1946.

Hopkins, Jeffrey. *Emptiness in the Mind-Only School of Buddhism.* Berkeley: University of California Press, 1999.

———. *Maps of the Profound: Jam-yang-shay-ba's* Great Exposition of Buddhist and Non-Buddhist Views on the Nature of Reality. Ithaca, N. Y.: Snow Lion Publications, 2003.

———. *Meditation on Emptiness.* London: Wisdom Publications, 1983.

———. *Tantra in Tibet: The Great Exposition of Secret Mantra by Tsong-ka-pa.* London: George Allen & Unwin, 1977.

Hopkins, Jeffrey, trans. *The Precious Garland and The Song of the Four Mindfulnesses.* New York: Harper and Row, 1975.

Horner, I. B., trans. *Cullavagga: The Book of the Discipline (Vinaya-piṭaka).* Vol. 5. London: Pali Text Society, 1952.

———. *Middle Length Sayings (Majjhima-Nikāya).* London: Pali Text Society, 1954.

Houben, Jan E. M. *The Sambandha-samuddeśa (Chapter on Relation) and Bhartṛhari's Philosophy of Language: A Study of Bhartṛhari's Sambandha-samuddeśa in the Context of the Vākyapadīya, with a Translation of Helārāja's Commentary Prakīrṇa-prakāśa.* Groningen: E. Forsten, 1995.

Houben, Jan E. M., ed. *Ideology and Status of Sanskrit: Contributions to the History of the Sanskrit Language.* Leiden: E. J. Brill, 1996.

Huth, Georg, ed. and trans. *Geschichte des Buddhismus in der Mongolei* [by Jigmay Namkha]. 2 vols. Strassburg: Karl J. Trübner, 1896.

Iida, Shotaro. "An Introduction to Svātantrika-Mādhyamika." Ph.D. dissertation, University of Wisconsin, 1968.

Instituut Kern. *India Antiqua: A Volume of Oriental Studies Presented by His Friends and Pupils to Jean Philippe Vogel, C. I. E., on the Occasion of the Fiftieth Anniversary of His Doctorate.* Leyden: E. J. Brill, 1947.

Iyer, K. A. Subramania, ed. *Vākyapadīya of Bhartṛhari (with the Commentary of Helārāja).* 2 vols. Poona: Deccan College, Postgraduate and Research Institute, 1963-1973.

Jaimini. *Mīmāmsā-darśane.* 6 vols. Ānandāśrama Sanskrit Series. Poona: Ānandāśrama mudramālaya, 1929-34.

Jaini, Padmanabh S. "On the 'Sarvajñatva' (Omniscience) of Mahāvira and the Buddha." In *Buddhist Studies in Honour of I. B. Horner,* ed. L. Cousins et al., pp. 71-90. Dordrecht: D. Reidel, 1974.

———. "The Vaibhāṣika Theory of Words and Meanings." *Bulletin of the School of Oriental and African Studies* 22 (1959): 95-107.

Jaini, Padmanabh S., ed. *Abhidharmadīpa with Vibhāṣāprabhāvṛtti.* Patna: Kashi Prasad Jayaswal Research Institute, 1977.

Jamyang Shayba ('Jam-dbyangs-bzhad-pa'i-rdo-rje). *Grub mtha'i rnam par bzhag pa 'khul spong gdong lnga'i sgra dbyang kun mkhyen lam bzang gsal ba'i rin chen sgron me.* In *The Collected Works of 'Jam-dbyaṅs-bźad-pa'i-rdo-rje, Reproduced from Prints from the Bkra-śis-'khyil Blocks.* Vol. 14. New Delhi: Ngawang Gelek Demo, 1973.

———. *Grub mtha'i rnam bshad rang gzhan grub mtha' kun dang zab don mchog tu gsal ba kun gzang zhing gi nyi ma lung rigs rgya mtsho skye dgu'i re ba kun skyong.* Musoorie: Dalama, 1962.

Jayatilleke, Kulatissa Nanda. *Early Buddhist Theory of Knowledge.* London: George Allen & Unwin, 1963.

Jetāri. *Sugatagranthamatavibhaṅgakārikā.* P5867, vol. 146.

———. *Sugatagranthamatavibhaṅgabhāṣya.* P5868, vol. 146.

Jha, Gaganatha, ed. and trans. *Shabara-Bhāṣya.* Vol. 1. Baroda: Oriental Institute, 1933.

Jñānagarbha. *Satyadvayavibhaṅga.* Not in P; Toh. 3881.

Jones, J. J., trans. *The Mahāvastu.* 3 vols. London: Pali Text Society, 1949-56.

Karunadasa, Yakupitiyage. *Buddhist Analysis of Matter.* Colombo: Department of Cultural Affairs, 1967.

Kielhorn, Franz. *Mahābhāṣya of Patañjali: Vyākaraṇa-mahābhāṣya.* Vol. 1. Bombay: 1880.

———. "On Śisupalavadha, II, 112." *Journal of the Royal Asiatic Society,* new series, 34 (1908): 499-502.

Kimura, Ryukan. *A Historical Study of the Terms Hīnayāna and Mahāyāna and the Origin of Mahāyāna Buddhism.* Calcutta: University of Calcutta, 1927.

Krishnamurti, Bhadriraju, ed. *Studies in Indian Linguistics: Prof. M. B. Emenau Ṣaṣṭipūrti Volume.* Poona: Centres of Advanced Study in Linguistics, 1968.

Kunjunni Raja, K. *Indian Theories of Meaning.* Madras: Adyar Library and Research Center, 1969.

Lamotte, Étienne. "La critique d'authenticité dans le bouddhisme." In Instituut Kern, *India Antiqua*, pp. 213-222.

———. "La critique d'interprétation dans le bouddhisme." *Annuaire de l'Institut de philologie et d'histoire orientales et slaves* 9 (1949): 341-361.

———. *Histoire du bouddhisme indien des origines a l'ère Śaka.* Louvain: Institut orientaliste, Bibliothèque de l'Univérsité, 1967.

———. "Passions and Impregnations of the Passions in Buddhism." In *Buddhist Studies in Honour of I. B. Horner*, ed. L. Cousins et al., pp. 91-104. Dordrecht: D. Reidel, 1974.

———. "Sur la formation du Mahāyāna." In *Asiatica: Festschrift Friedrich Weller*, pp. 377-396. Leipzig: Otto Harrassowitz, 1954.

———. *The Teaching of Vimalakīrti.* Trans. Sara Boin. London: Pali Text Society, 1976.

———. *Le traité de la grande vertue de sagesse. Mahāprajñāpāramitāśāstra.* 3 vols. Louvain: Institut orientaliste, Bibliothèque de l'Univérsité, 1966.

Lati Rinbochay and Elizabeth Napper. *Mind in Tibetan Buddhism.* Valois, N.Y.: Gabriel/Snow Lion, 1980.

La Vallée Poussin, Louis de. "Documents d'Abhidharma." *Bulletin de l'École française d'Extrême-Orient* 30 (1930): 247-298.

———. "Documents d'Abhidharma: La controverse du temps." *Mélanges chinois et bouddhiques* 5 (1937): 7-158.

———. "Documents d'Abhidharma: Les deux, les quatre, les trois vérités," *Mélanges chinois et bouddhiques* 5 (1937): 159-187.

La Vallée Poussin, Louis de, ed. *Madhyamakāvatāra par Candrakīrti.* St. Petersburg: Imprimerie de l'Académie impériale des sciences, 1912.

———. *Mūlamadhyamakakārikās de Nāgārjuna avec la Prasannapadā commentaire de Candrakīrti.* St. Petersburg: Imprimerie de l'Académie impériale des sciences, 1903-1913.

La Vallée Poussin, Louis de, trans. *L'Abhidharmakośa de Vasubandhu.* 6 vols. Brussels: Institut belge des hautes études chinoises, 1980.

———. *Vijñaptimātratāsiddhi: La Siddhi de Hiuan-tsang.* 2 vols. and index. Paris: Paul Geuthner, 1928-1948.

Law, Bimala Churn, trans. *The Debates Commentary (Kathāvatthuppakaraṇa-Aṭṭhakathā).* London: Pali Text Society, 1969.

Leclère, Adhémard. *Les livres sacrés du Cambodge.* Annales du Musée Guimet, Bibliothèque d'études, vol. 20. Paris: Ernest Leroux, 1906.

Lefman, Salomon, ed. *Lalita Vistara: Leben und Lehre des Çâkya-Buddha.* 2 vols. Heidelberg: Halle A. S., 1902-08.

Lévi, Sylvain. "Sur la recitation primitive des textes bouddhiques." *Journal Asiatique* 1 (1915): 401-447.

Lin Li-Kouang. *L'Aide-Mémoire de la Vraie Loi: Saddharma-smṛtyupasthāna-sūtra.* Paris: Adrien-Maisonneuve, 1949.

Mahābhāṣya. See Kielhorn.

Maitreya. *Madhyānta-vibhaṅga.* P5522, vol. 108. See also Pandeya.

Majjhima-Nikāya. See Trenckner and Horner.

Malalasekera, George Peiris. *The Pāli Literature of Ceylon.* London: Royal Asiatic Society of Great Britain and Ireland, 1928.

Masuda, Jiryo. "Origin and Doctrines of Early Indian Buddhist Schools: A Translation of the Hsüan-chwang Version of Vasumitra's Treatise." *Asia Major* 2 (1925): 1-78.

Mazumdar, Pradip Kumar. *The Philosophy of Language: In the Light of Pāṇinian and the Mīmāṃsaka Schools of Indian Philosophy.* Calcutta: Sanskrit Pustak Bhandar, 1977.

McDermott, A. Charlene. "The Sautrāntika Arguments against the *Traikālyavāda* in the Light of the Contemporary Tense Revolution." *Philosophy East and West* 24 (1974): 194-200.

Miller, Robert James. *Monasteries and Culture Change in Inner Mongolia.* Wiesbaden: O. Harrassowitz, 1959.

Morris, Richard, and Edmund Hardy, eds. *Aṅguttara-nikāya.* London: Pali Text Society, 1955.

Müller, Friedrich Max, ed. *Aṭṭhasālinī.* London: Pali Text Society, 1897.

Müller, Friedrich Max, ed. and trans. *The Dharmapada.* Oxford: Clarendon Press, 1881.

Murti, T[irupattur] R[ameseshayyer] V[enkatachala]. *The Central Philosophy of Buddhism.* London: George Allen & Unwin, 1970.

Nāgārjuna. *Mūlamadhyamakakārikā / Madhyamakaśāstra.* P5224, vol. 95; also see La Vallée Poussin.

———. *Ratnāvalī.* P5658, vol. 129; also see Hopkins.

Ñāṇamoli, Bhikkhu, trans. *The Guide (Nettippakaraṇa).* London: Pali Text Society, 1962.

———. *Piṭaka-Disclosure (Peṭakopadesa).* London: Pali Text Society, 1949.

———. *The Path of Purification: Visuddhimagga.* Colombo: A. Semage, 1964.

Nārada, Thera, trans. *The Dhammapada.* London: John Murray, 1954.

Neumann, Karl Eugen. *Die Reden Gotamo Buddhos aus der mittlere Sammlung Majjhimanikāyo des Pāli-Kanons.* 3 vols. Munich: R. Piper & Company, 1922.

Newland, Guy. *Appearance and Reality: The Two Truths in the Four Buddhist Tenet Systems.* Ithaca, N. Y.: Snow Lion Publications, 1999.

———. *The Two Truths in the Mādhyamika Philosophy of the Ge-luk-ba Order of Tibetan Buddhism.* Ithaca, N. Y.: Snow Lion Publications, 1992.

Ngawang Belden (Ngag-dbang dPal-ldan). *Grub mtha' chen mo'i mchan 'grel dka' gnad mdud grol blo gsal gces nor.* Sarnath: Pleasure of Elegant Sayings Printing Press, 1964.

———. *Grub mtha' bzhi'i lugs kyi kun rdzob dang don dam pa'i don rnam par bshad pa legs bshad dpyid kyi dpal mo'i dbyang.* New Delhi: Lama Guru Deva, 1972.

Norman, Harry Campbell, ed. *Dhammapadāṭṭhakathā.* London: Pali Text Society, 1906.

Nyanatiloka, Bhikkhu. *Guide through the Abhidhamma-Piṭaka.* Kandy: Buddhist Publications Society, 1971.

Obermiller, Eugéne, trans. *History of Buddhism (Chos-ḥbyung) by Bu-ston* [*bDe bar gshegs pa'i bstan pa'i gsal byed chos kyi 'byung gnas gsung rab rin po che'i mdzod*]. 2 vols. Heidelberg: O. Harrassowitz, 1931-32.

Oldenberg, Hermann, ed. *The Cullavagga.* London: Williams and Norgate, 1880.

Oldenberg, Hermann, ed. and trans. *Dīpavaṃsa: An Ancient Buddhist Historical Record.* London: Williams and Norgate, 1879.

Pande, Govind Chandra. *Studies in the Origins of Buddhism.* Allahabad: University of Allahabad, 1957.

Pandey, Raj Bali. *Indian Palaeography.* Benares: Motilal Banarasi Das, 1952.

Pandeya, Ram Chandra, ed. *Madhyānta-Vibhāga-Śāstra* [with *Bhāṣya* of Vasubandhu and *Ṭīkā* of Sthiramati]. Delhi: Motilal Banarsidass, 1969.

Patañjali. *Mahābhāṣya.* See Kielhorn.

Patnaik, Tandra. *Śabda: A Study of Bhartṛhari's Philosophy of Language.* New Delhi: D. K. Printworld, 1994.

Pischel, Richard. *Comparative Grammar of the Prakrit Languages.* Trans. Subhandra Jha. Delhi: Motilal Banarsidass, 1965.

Pitāputrasamāgama-sūtra. P760.16, vol. 23.

Potter, Karl H. *Indian Metaphysics and Epistemology: The Tradition of Nyāya-Vaiśeṣika up to Gangeśa.* Princeton: Princeton University Press, 1977.

Pradhan, Pralhad. "The First Pārājika of the Dharmaguptaka-Vinaya and the Pali Sutta-Vibhaṅga." *Viśva-Bharati Annals* 1 (1945): 1-34.

Pradhan, Pralhad [i.e., Prahallad], ed. *Ācārya Vasubandhu Pranītam Abhidharmakośabhāṣyam.* Patna: K. P. Jayaswal Research Institute, 1967.

———. *Abhidharma Samuccaya of Asanga.* Santiniketan: Viśva-Bharati, 1950.

Prebish, Charles S., ed. *Buddhist Monastic Discipline: The Sanskrit Pratimokṣa Sūtras of the Mahāsāṃghikas and Mūlasarvāstivādins.* University Park: Pennsylvania State University Press, 1975.

Prebish, Charles S., and Janice J. Nattier. "Mahāsāṃghika Origins: The Beginnings of Buddhist Sectarianism," *History of Religions* 16 (1977): 237-272.

Przyluski, Jean. *Le concile de Rājagṛha; introduction à l'histoire des canons et des sectes bouddhiques.* Paris: Paul Geuthner, 1926.

Pūrṇavardhana. *Abhidharmakośaṭīkālakṣaṇānusārinī.* P5594, vol. 118.

Rahula, Walpola, trans. *Abhidharmasamuccaya.* Paris: École française d'Extrême-Orient, 1971.

Rath, Gayatri. *Linguistic Philosophy in Vākyapadīya.* New Delhi: Bharatiya Vidya Prakashan, 2000.

Renou, Louis, and Jean Filliozat. *L'Inde Classique.* Vol. 2. Paris: Imprimerie Nationale, 1953.

Rhys Davids, Caroline Augusta Foley, ed. *The Aṅguttara Nikāya.* 6 vols. London: Pali Text Society, 1885-1932.

———. *Yamaka.* 2 vols. London: Pali Text Society, 1911-1913.

———. *Yamaka-aṭṭhakathā* ["The Yamaka Commentary from the Pañcappakaranatthakathā"]. In *Journal of the Pali Text Society* 6 (1910-12).

Rhys Davids, Caroline A. F., trans. *The Milinda Questions.* London: George Routledge & Sons, 1930.

———. *The Book of the Kindred Sayings* [*Saṃyutta-nikāya*]. 5 vols. Oxford: University Press, 1917-1930.

Rhys Davids, Thomas W., trans. *The Questions of King Milinda.* Oxford: Clarendon Press, 1890.

Rhys Davids, Thomas W., and Caroline A. F., trans. *Dialogues of the Buddha* [*Dīgha-nikāya*]. 3 vols. London: Pali Text Society, 1899-1921.

Rhys Davids, Thomas W., and J. Estlin Carpenter, eds. *The Dīgha Nikāya.* 3 vols. London: Pali Text Society, 1889, 1903, 1911.

Rhys Davids, Thomas W., and William Stede. *The Pali Text Society's Pali-English Dictionary.* Repr., London: Pali Text Society, 1972.

Rhys Davids, Thomas W., and Hermann Oldenberg, trans. *Vinaya Texts.* 3 vols. Oxford: Clarendon Press, 1881-85.

Ruegg, David Seyfort. *Contributions à l'histoire de la philosophie linguistique indienne.* Paris: Publications de l'institut de civilisation indienne, 1959.

Sadaw, Ledi. "Some Points in Buddhist Doctrine." *Journal of the Pali Text Society* 7 (1914): 115-163.

Samādhirājasūtra. P795, vols. 31-32.

Saṃyutta-nikāya. See Feer and C. Rhys Davids.

Sanjdorj, M[agsarjavyn]. *Manchu Chinese Colonial Rule in Northern Mongolia.* New York: St. Martin's Press, 1968.

Śāntarakṣita. *Madhyamakālaṃkāra.* P5284, vol. 99.

———. *Madhyamakālaṃkāravṛtti.* P5285, vol. 99.

Śāntideva. *Bodhisattvacaryāvatāra.* P5272, vol. 99.

Scharf, Peter M. *The Denotation of Generic Terms in Ancient Indian Philosophy: Grammar, Nyāya and Mīmāṃsā.* Philadelphia: American Philosophical Society, 1996.

Schayer, Stanislaw. "Precanonical Buddhism." *Archiv Orientální* 7 (1935): 121-132.

Sharma, Dhirendra. *The Differentiation Theory of Meaning in Indian Logic.* The Hague: Mouton, 1969.

Shwe Zan Aung and Caroline A. F. Rhys Davids, trans. *Points of Controversy* [*Kathāvatthu* of Moggaliputta Tissa]. London: Pali Text Society, 1915.

Singh, Sanghasen, ed. *Sarvāstivāda and Its Traditions.* Delhi: Department of Buddhist Studies, 1994.

Sopa, Geshe Lhundup, and Jeffrey Hopkins. *Practice and Theory of Tibetan Buddhism.* New York: Grove Press, 1976.

Sprung, Mervyn, ed. *The Problem of Two Truths in Buddhism and Vedanta.* Dordrecht: D. Reidel, 1973.

Staal, Johan Frits. *A Reader in the Sanskrit Grammarians.* Cambridge: MIT Press, 1972.

Stcherbatsky, Theodore. *Buddhist Logic.* 2 vols. Repr., New York: Dover, 1962.

———. *The Central Conception of Buddhism and the Meaning of the Word "Dharma."* Repr., Calcutta: S. Gupta, 1961.

Sutta-Nipāta. See Chalmers; also Andersen and Smith.

Suzuki, Daisetz Teitaro, et al., eds. *The Tibetan Tripitaka, Peking Edition.* Tokyo: Tibetan Tripitaka Research Institute, 1956.

Takakusu, Junjirō. *A Record of the Buddhist Religion as Practised in India and the Malay Archipelago (A. D. 671-695) by I-tsing.* Repr., Delhi: Munshiram Manoharlal, 1966.

Tāranātha. *History of Buddhism.* See Chimpa.

Taylor, Arnold C., ed. *Kathāvatthu.* London: Pali Text Society, 1894-97.

Tin Pe Maung, trans.; Caroline A. F. Rhys Davis, ed. *The Expositor (Aṭṭhasālinī), Buddhaghosa's Commentary on the Dhammasaṅganī, The First Book of the Abhidhamma Piṭaka.* 2 vols. London: Pali Text Society, 1920-21.

Tōhoku Daigaku, Hōbungakubu. See Ui.

Trenckner, Vilhelm, ed. *Majjhima-Nikāya.* London: Pali Text Society, 1948.

———. *The Milindapañho.* London: Royal Asiatic Society, 1928.

Tsongkhapa. *dbU ma la 'jug pa'i rgya cher bshad pa dgongs pa rab gsal.* P6143, vol. 154.

———. *dbU ma rtsa ba'i tshig le'ur byas ba shes rab ces bya ba'i rnam bshad rigs pa'i rgya mtsho.* P6153, vol. 156; also, Varanasi: Pleasure of Elegant Sayings Printing Press, 1973.

———. *Drang ba dang nges pa'i don rnam par phye ba'i bstan bcos legs bshad snying po.* P6142, vol. 153.

———. *Lam rim chen mo.* P6001, vol. 152.

———. *Legs bshad gser gyi phreng ba shes rab kyi pha rol tu phyin pa'i man ngag gi bstan bcos mngon par rtogs pa'i rgyan 'grel pa dang bcas pa'i rgya cher bshad pa.* P6150, vol. 154.

———. *Sang rgyas bcom ldan 'das la zab mo rten cing 'brel bar 'byung ba gsung ba'i sgo nas bstod pa legs par bshad pa'i snying po.* P6016, vol. 153.

Tucci, Giuseppe. *The Religions of Tibet.* Trans. Geoffrey Samuel. Repr., Bombay: Allied Publishers, 1980.

Ui, Hakuju, et al., eds. *A Complete Catalogue of the Tibetan Buddhist Canons* [*Chibetto Daizōkyō sōmokuroku*]. Sendai: Tōhoku Imperial University, 1934.

van Buitenen, J. A. B. "Speculations on the Name 'Satyam' in the Upaniṣads." In *Studies in Indian Linguistics*, ed. B. Krishnamurti, pp. 54-61. Poona: Linguistic Society of India, 1968.

van Gulik, Robert Hans. *Siddham: An Essay on the History of Sanskrit Study in China and Japan.* Nagpur: International Academy of Indian Culture, 1956.

Vasubandhu. *Abhidharmakośa.* P5590, vol. 115.

———. *Abhidharmakośabhāṣya.* P5591, vol. 115; also see Pradhan and La Vallée Poussin.

———. *Vyākhyāyukti.* P5562, vol. 113.

Vijaya Rani. *The Buddhist Philosophy as Presented in Mīmāṃsā-śloka-vārttika.* Delhi: Parimal Publications, 1982.

Vogel, Claus, ed. *Jñanamuktāvalī: Commemoration Volume in Honour of Johannes Nobel, on the Occasion of His 70th Birthday, Offered by Pupils and Colleagues.* Lahore: International Academy of Indian Culture, 1959.

Vostrikov, Andrei Ivanovich. "Some Corrections and Critical Remarks on Dr. Johan van Manem's Contribution to the Bibliography of Tibet." *Bulletin of the School of Oriental Studies* 8 (1935): 51-76.

———. *Tibetan Historical Literature.* Trans. Harish Chandra Gupta. Calcutta: Indian Studies Past and Present, 1970.

Waddell, L. Austine. *The Buddhism of Tibet or Lamaism.* Repr., Cambridge: W. Heffer and Sons, 1971.

Waldschmit, Ernst. "Zum ersten buddhistischen Konzil in Rājagṛha." In *Asiatica: Festschrift Friedrich Weller,* ed. Johannes Schubert, pp. 817-828. Leipzig: Otto Harrassowitz, 1954.

Walleser, Max, ed. *Manoratha-pūraṇī: Buddhaghosa's Commentary on the Aṅguttara-nikāya.* Vol. 1. London: Pali Text Society, 1973.

Warder, Anthony K. "The Earliest Indian Logic." *Trudi XXV Mezhdunarodnogo Kongressa Vostokovedov* 4 (1963): 56-68.

———. *Indian Buddhism.* Delhi: Motilal Banarsidass, 1980.

Warder, A. K., and Buddhadatta, A. P., eds. *Mohavicchedanī: Abhidhammamātikāṭṭhavaṇṇaṇa.* London: Pali Text Society, 1961.

Whitney, William Dwight. *Sanskrit Grammar.* 2nd ed. Repr., Cambridge, Mass.: Harvard University Press, 1967.

Willemen, Charles, trans. *The Essence of Metaphysics: Abhidharmahṛdaya.* Brussels: L'institut belge des hautes études bouddiques, 1975.

Willemen, Charles, Bart Dessein, and Collett Cox, eds. *Sarvāstivāda Buddhist Scholasticism.* Leiden: E. J. Brill, 1998.

Williams, Paul M. "On the Abhidharma Ontology." *Journal of Indian Philosophy* 9 (1980): 229-257.

Winternitz, Maurice. *A History of Indian Literature.* Vol. 2. Calcutta: University of Calcutta, 1933.

Wogihara, Unrai, ed. *Sphuṭārthābhidharmakośavyākhyā of Yaśomitra.* Repr., Osnabrück: Biblio Verlag, 1970.

Woodruffe, Sir John. *The Garland of Letters.* Repr., Madras: Ganesh and Co., 1974.

Woodward, Frank L., and Edward M. Hare, trans. *The Book of Gradual Sayings (Aṅguttara-nikāya).* 3 vols. London: Pali Text Society, 1932.

Yaśomitra. *Abhidharmakośavyākhyāsphuṭārtha.* P5593, vol. 116; also see Wogihara.

Notes

1 Recent scholarship on the Vaibhāṣikas includes Charles Willemen, Bart Dessein, and Collett Cox, *Sarvāstivāda Buddhist Scholasticism* (New York: E. J. Brill, 1998) and Sanghasen Singh, ed., *Sarvāstivāda and Its Traditions* (Delhi: Department of Buddhist Studies, 1994).

2 Such as Daniel Cozort, *Unique Tenets of the Middle Way Consequence School* (Ithaca, N. Y.: Snow Lion Publications, 1998); Daniel Cozort and Craig Preston, *Buddhist Philosophy: Losang Gönchok's Short Commentary to Jamyang Shayba's* Root Text on Tenets (Ithaca, N.Y.: Snow Lion Publications, 2003); Guy Newland, *The Two Truths in the Mādhyamika Philosophy of the Ge-luk-ba Order of Tibetan Buddhism* (Ithaca, N.Y.: Snow Lion Publications, 1992); and Jeffrey Hopkins, *Maps of the Profound: Jam-yang-shay-ba's* Great Exposition of Buddhist and Non-Buddhist Views on the Nature of Reality (Ithaca, N.Y.: Snow Lion Publications, 2003).

3 Quoted by Bu-dön in his *History of Buddhism (Chos-ḥbyung) by Bu-ston*, trans. Eugéne Obermiller (Heidelberg: O. Harrassowitz, 1931-32), Part 2, pp. 166-167.

4 Prabhat Chandra Chakravarti, *The Philosophy of Sanskrit Grammar* (University of Calcutta, 1930), pp. 10ff.

5 Jules Bloch, *Indo-Aryan: From the Vedas to the Modern Times*, trans. Alfred Meister (Paris: Adrien-Maisonneuve, 1965), pp. 23ff. The importance of proper pronunciation for the ritual effectiveness of the Vedic sacrifice is discussed in Madeleine Biardeau, *Théorie de la connaissance et philosophie de la parole dans le brahmanisme classique* (Paris: Mouton, 1964), p. 34, citing Patañjali's *Mahābhāṣya* 1.1.14. For more on the issue of the religious authority of Sanskrit, see Madhav M. Deshpande and Peter Edwin Hook, eds., *Aryan and Non-Aryan in India* (Ann Arbor: University of Michigan Press, 1979).

6 Thomas Burrow, *The Sanskrit Language* (London: Faber and Faber, 1966), pp. 47-48.

7 For variants of this story, see Lama Chimpa and Alaka Chattopadhyaya, trans., *Tāranātha's History of Buddhism in India* (Simla: Indian Institute of Advanced Study, 1970), p. 11; Bu-ston, pp. 167-168; and J. Frits Staal, *A Reader in the Sanskrit Grammarians* (Cambridge, Mass.: MIT Press, 1972), p. 22.

8 The ancient Chinese pilgrim I-tsing, who traveled to India, wrote in his journal that Patañjali's *Mahābhāṣya* and Bhartṛhari's *Vākyapadīya* were included in the curriculum of study for the monks at the Buddhist monastery at Nalanda. See Junjirō Takakusu, *A Record of the Buddhist Religion as Practised in India and the Malay Archipelago (A. D. 671-695) by I-tsing* (Delhi: Munshiram Manoharlal, 1966), p. 76. The study of grammar was continued in the monastic centers of Tibet.

9 Quoted in Chakravarti, *Philosophy*, pp. 16-17, from Bhartṛhari's *Vākyapadīya*; see K. A. Subramania Iyer, ed., *Vākyapadīya of Bhartṛhari, with the Commentary of Helārāja,*

Kaṇḍa III, 2 vols. (Poona: Deccan College, Postgraduate and Research Institute, 1963-73).

10 Quoted in Franz Kielhorn, "On Śisupalavadha, II, 112," *Journal of the Royal Asiatic Society*, new series, 34 (1908): 501.

11 Burrow, *The Sanskrit Language*, pp. 41-42; Bishnupada Bhattacharya, *Yāska's Nirukta and the Science of Etymology* (Calcutta: Firma K. L. Mukhopadhyay, 1958), p. 44; J. A. B. van Buitenen, "Speculations on the Name 'Satyam' in the Upaniṣads," in *Studies in Indian Linguistics: Professor M. B. Emeneau Saṣṭipūrti Volume*, ed. Bhadriya Krishnamurti (Poona: Linguistic Society of India, 1968), pp. 54-61; Prabhat Chandra Chakravarti, *Linguistic Speculations of the Hindus* (Calcutta: University of Calcutta, 1933), Intro.

12 Bhattacharya, *Yāska's Nirukta*, p. 44; Dhirendra Sharma, *The Differentiation Theory of Meaning in Indian Logic* (The Hague: Mouton, 1969), pp. 45-46; Stanislaw Schayer, "Precanonical Buddhism," *Archiv Orientální* 7 (1935): 129 n.; Karl Eugen Neumann, *Die Reden Gotamo Buddhos aus der mittlere Sammlung Majjhimanikāyo des Pāli-Kanons* (Munich: R. Piper, 1922), vol. 1, preface, cited by Maurice Winternitz, *A History of Indian Literature* (Calcutta: University of Calcutta, 1933), vol. 2, pp. 204-205.

13 Biardeau, *Théorie de la connaissance et philosophie*, pp. 36-37.

14 Biardeau, *Théorie de la connaissance et philosophie*, pp. 41-43; Biardeau feels that his distinction between the two ultimately fails. Padmanabh S. Jaini, in "The Vaibhāṣika Theory of Words and Meanings," *Bulletin of the School of Oriental and African Studies* 22 (1959): 107, notes the ridicule that the Vaibhāṣika author of the *Abhidharmadīpa* directs at the *sphoṭa* theory.

15 Karl H. Potter, *Indian Metaphysics and Epistemology: The Tradition of Nyāya-Vaiśeṣika up to Gangeśa* (Princeton: Princeton University Press, 1977), pp. 152-153.

16 Sir John Woodruffe, *The Garland of Letters*, Repr. (Madras: Ganesh and Company, 1974), and Robert Hans van Gulik, *Siddham: An Essay on the History of Sanskrit Studies in China and Japan* (Nagpur: International Academy of Indian Culture, 1956).

17 Quoted in Chakravarti, *Philosophy*, p. 17.

18 David Seyfort Ruegg, *Contributions à l'histoire de la philosophie linguistique indienne* (Paris: Publications de l'institut de civilisation indienne, 1959), pp. 61ff.; Paul Hacker, *Vivarta: Studien zur Geschichte der illusionistischen Kosmologie und Erkenntnistheorie der Inder* (Mainz: Verlag der Wissenschaften und der Literatur, 1953), p. 204; Radhika Herzberger, *Bhartṛhari and the Buddhists: An Essay in the Development of Fifth and Sixth Century Indian Thought* (Dordrecht: D. Reidel, 1986); Tandra Patnaik, *Śabda: A Study of Bhartṛhari's Philosophy of Language* (New Delhi: D. K. Printworld, 1994); Gayatri Rath, *Linguistic Philosophy in Vākyapadīya* (New Delhi: Bharatiya Vidya Prakashan, 2000).

19 Anthony K. Warder, *Indian Buddhism* (Delhi: Motilal Banarsidass, 1980), pp. 464-465; see also A. Charlene McDermott, "The Sautrāntika Arguments against the *Traikālyavāda* in the Light of the Contemporary Tense Revolution," *Philosophy East and West* 24 (1974): 194-200; Harold G. Coward and K. Kunjunni Raja, eds., *The Philosophy of the Grammarians* (Princeton: Princeton University Press, 1990); Vijaya

Rani, *The Buddhist Philosophy as Presented in Mīmāṃsā-śloka-vārttika* (Delhi: Parimal Publications, 1982); Peter M. Scharf, *The Denotation of Generic Terms in Ancient Indian Philosophy: Grammar, Nyāya and Mīmāṃsā* (Philadelphia: American Philosophical Society, 1996); Othmar Gächter, *Hermeneutics and Language in Pūrva Mīmāṃsā: A Study in Śābara Bhāṣya* (Delhi: Motilal Banarsidass, 1983); Pradip Kumar Mazumdar, *The Philosophy of Language in the Light of Pāṇinian and the Mīmāṃsaka Schools of Indian Philosophy* (Calcutta: Sanskrit Pustak Bhandar, 1977); R. C. Dwivedi, ed., *Studies in Mīmāṃsā: Dr. Mandan Mishra Felicitation Volume* (Delhi: Motilal Banarsidass, 1994).

20 Étienne Lamotte, *Histoire du bouddhisme indien des origines à l'ère Śaka* (Louvain: Institut orientaliste, Bibliothèque de l'Université, 1967), pp. 608-614; Lin Li-Kouang, *L'Aide-Mémoire de la Vraie Loi: Saddharma-smṛtyupasthana-sūtra*, Musée Guimet, Bibliothèque d'Études 54 (Paris: Adrien-Maisonneuve, 1949), pp. 216-227.

21 Jan E. M. Houben, *The Sambandha-samuddeśa (Chapter on Relation) and Bhartṛhari's Philosophy of Language: A Study of Bhartṛhari's Sambandha-samuddeśa in the Context of the Vākyapadīya, with a Translation of Helārāja's Commentary Prakīrna-prakāśa* (Groningen: E. Forsten, 1995).

22 Paraphrased from Richard Pischel, *Comparative Grammar of the Prakrit Languages*, trans. Subhandra Jha (Delhi: Motilal Banarsidass, 1965), p. 15.

23 According to Prabodh Chandra Bagchi, "Fundamental Problems of the Origins of Buddhism," *France-Asie/Asia* 17, no. 168 (July-August 1961): 2232-2233, 2238. Bagchi based his judgment partly on an analysis of the language of the Bhabra Rock Edict. He concluded that, "Sanskrit and Pali Buddhist literature both inherited an older literary tradition recorded in a dialect which is now lost." Pali's position in this is somewhat unclear. Lamotte, *Histoire*, pp. 614-617, summarized the debate on the place of Pali in Middle-Indic languages and the probability that what we know as Pali is not in fact the Māgadhī dialect which was the first language of the Buddhist scriptures. See also Jules Bloch, *Indo-Aryan*, pp. 10ff. On the Buddhists' canon formation, see the article by Ronald M. Davidson, "An Introduction to the Standards of Scriptural Authenticity in Indian Buddhism," in *Chinese Buddhist Apocrypha*, ed. Robert E. Buswell (Honolulu: University of Hawai'i Press, 1990), pp. 291-325.

24 *Dīgha-Nikāya* 2.109, trans. by I. B. Horner, in Edward Conze, ed., *Buddhist Texts through the Ages* (New York: Harper and Row, 1964), p. 103.

25 Lamotte, *Histoire*, pp. 608-610.

26 Lamotte, *Histoire*, pp. 612, 622-628; also Lin Li-Kouang, *L'Aide-Mémoire*, pp. 219-220. The story is also in the Pali canon—*Cullavagga* 5.33 and *Vinaya* 2.139ff. Franklin Edgerton, *Buddhist Hybrid Sanskrit Grammar and Dictionary*, vol. 1 (Delhi: Motilal Banarsidass, 1972), pp. 1-2, points out that the Buddha's meaning in this story is disputed, both in ancient sources and in modern attempts to understand the Buddha's admonition. For example, the Buddha's statement in the Pali *Vinaya*, "I prescribe that you should learn the Buddha's words each in his own dialect" (*Aniyānāmi . . . sakāya niruttiyā buddhavacanam pariyāpunitum*), could be interpreted to mean that the Buddha wished them to learn the doctrine in *his* own, that is, the Buddha's own, dialect. The Theravāda exegete Buddhaghosa in fact took it in this sense and identified the Buddha's language as "Māgadhī," but understood this to mean what we call "Pali" (*Ettha sakā nirutti nāma sammāsambuddhena vuttappakāro Māgadhīko vohāro*).

27 Paul Demiéville, "*Bombai*," in Demiéville, ed., *Hōbōgirin: Dictionnaire encyclopedique du bouddhisme d'apres les sources chinoises et japonaises* (Tokyo: Maison Franco-Japonaise, 1929).

28 *Brāhmaṇavagga* (Chap. 26) in F. Max Müller, ed. and trans., *The Dharmapada* (Oxford: Clarendon Press, 1881), pp. 89ff.; an idea also found in the *Sutta-nipāta*, verses 648-650.

29 *Sutta-nipāta*, verses 903-904; Lord Robert Chalmers, *Buddha's Teachings* (Cambridge: Harvard University Press, 1931), pp. 216-217; John Brough, *The Gāndhārī Dharmapada* (London: Oxford University Press, 1962), p. 181.

30 A. L. Basham, *History and Doctrines of the Ājīvikas, A Vanished Indian Religion* (London: Luzac, 1951), compiled a list of technical terms that were common among the wandering religious ascetics of the Buddha's time, but which have come to be associated with Buddhism alone because of its greater success.

31 *Aṅgutta-nikāya* 4.163, Richard Morris and E. Hardy, eds. (London: Pali Text Society, 1955), pp. 188ff.; F. L. Woodward and E. M. Hare, *The Book of Gradual Sayings* (London: Pali Text Society, 1932); discussed in George Doherty Bond, "The Problem of Interpretation in Theravāda Buddhism and Christianity" (Ph.D. dissertation, Northwestern University, 1972), pp. 51-52.

32 *Majjhima-nikāya* 2.164-177, ed. Vilhelm Trenckner (London: Pali Text Society, 1948).

33 Padmanabh S. Jaini describes the growth of the *abhidharma* in detail in his introduction to the *Abhidharmadīpa with Vibhāṣāprabhāvṛtti* (Patna: Kashi Prasad Jayaswal Research Institute, 1977), pp. 22-67. Śāriputra's position as the "patron saint" of the *abhidharma* is clarified in the sources cited by Lamotte in *Histoire*, p. 219.

34 This story, recorded in *Vinaya Texts*, vol. 1, trans. by T. W. Rhys Davis and Hermann Oldenberg (Oxford: Clarendon Press, 1881), pp. 40-41, is discussed in Anthony K. Warder, *Indian Buddhism*, pp. 55-56, and in Ananda K. Coomaraswamy, "Some Pāli Words," *Harvard Journal of Asiatic Studies* 4 (1939): 173.

35 These passages are summarized in Étienne Lamotte, "La critique d'interprétation dans le bouddhisme," *Annuaire de l'Institut de philologie et d'histoire orientales et slaves* 9 (1949): 345-346.

36 The development of the *vinaya* texts and the accompanying confessional ceremony is treated in Charles Prebish, ed., *Buddhist Monastic Discipline: The Sanskrit Prātimokṣa Sūtras of the Mahāsāṃghikas and the Mūlasarvāstivādins* (University Park: Pennsylvania State University Press, 1975), pp. 17-28, and in Erich Frauwallner, *The Earliest Vinaya and the Beginnings of Buddhist Literature.* Serie Orientale Roma, vol. 8 (Rome: Is.M.E.O., 1956).

37 The collected doctrinal verses contained at least the *Arthapada*, which is the Pali *Atthavaggiya*, which shares verses with the *Sutta-nipāta*. The early existence of this collection is inferred from an incident in which the Buddha required one of his disciples to recite it, discussed by Sylvain Lévi, "Sur la récitation primitive des textes bouddhiques," *Journal Asiatique* 1 (1915): 401-447; by Étienne Lamotte, *Le traité de la grande vertue de sagesse (Mahāprajñāpāramitāśāstra)* (Louvain: Institut orientaliste, Bibliothèque de l'Université, 1966), vol. 1, pp. 39-40; by Lin Li-Kouang, *L'Aide-Mémoire de la Vraie Loi*, p. 224; and by Bagchi, "Fundamental Problems of the Origins of Buddhism," pp. 2234-2236.

38 Jaini, *Abhidharmadīpa*, p. 50.

39 Paraphrased from the translation in Prahallad Pradhan, "The First Pārājika of the Dharmaguptaka-Vinaya and the Pali Sutta-Vibhaṅga," *Viśva-Bharati Annals* 1 (1945): 22.

40 These sources are reviewed in Ernst Waldschmidt, "Zum ersten buddhistischen Konzil in Rājagṛha," *Asiatica: Festschrift Friedrich Weller* (Leipzig: Otto Harrassowitz, 1954), pp. 820-821; in Jean Przyluski, *Le concile de Rājagṛha* (Paris: Paul Geuthner, 1928), vol. 1, pp. 228ff.; and in Marcel Hofinger, *Étude sur le concile de Vaiśālī*. Bibliothèque du Muséon, vol. 20 (Louvain: Bureau du Muséon, 1946), p. 147.

41 Hofinger, *Étude sur le concile de Vaiśālī*, pp. 38, 147, 226.

42 These are from the *Catuḥ-pratisaraṇa-sūtra*, considered at length in Étienne Lamotte, "La critique d'interprétation dans le bouddhisme," *Annuaire de l'Institut de philologie et d'histoire orientales et slaves* 9 (1949): 341-342. He surmises that the sūtra is a fairly late composition; however, the four reliances are cited in the *Abhidharmakośa* (LVP, chap. 9, p. 246), the *Abhidharmakośa-vyākhyā*, the *Akṣayamatinirdeśa-sūtra*, the *Dharmasaṃgraha*, the *Bodhisattvabhūmi*, and the *Sūtrālaṃkāra*.

43 Perhaps the Sarvāstivāda School was responsible for this objectification of "truths" which certainly spread to other schools, including those that were disseminated to Tibet; La Vallée Poussin, "Documents d'Abhidharma: Les deux, les quatre, les trois vérités," *Mélanges chinois et bouddhiques* 5 (1937): 173 n. The Theravāda School does not treat the four truths as objects in this sense.

44 Jaini, *Abhidharmadīpa*, Intro. and p. 50, discusses the evolution of the *abhidharma* collection from these *mātṛkā*, as does A. K. Warder in "The Mātikā," in A. K. Warder and A. P. Buddhadatta, eds., *Mohavicchedanī: Abhidhammamātikāṭṭhavaṇṇaṇa* (London: Pali Text Society, 1961) pp. xixff.; by Hofinger, *Étude sur le concile de Vaiśālī*, p. 230; and in T. W. Rhys Davis and William Stede, *The Pali Text Society's Pali-English Dictionary*, Repr. (London: Pali Text Society, 1972), p. 337.

45 Various etymologies were given for *abhidharma*, which led to such meanings as "clear doctrine," "concerning the doctrine," "research into the doctrine," and even, according to Yaśomitra's *Abhidharmakośavyākhyā*, "higher knowledge." The meaning of "higher doctrine" is given by Buddhaghosa in the *Aṭṭhasālinī*; see P. Maung Tin, trans., Caroline Rhys Davis, ed., *The Expositor: Buddhaghosa's Commentary on the Dhammasaṅganī* (London: Pali Text Society, 1920), vol. 1, pp. 3-4: "Herein, what is meant by 'Abhidhamma'? That which exceeds and is distinguished from the Dhamma (the Suttas).... This 'dhamma' is called Abhidhamma because it excels and is distinguished by several qualities from the other Dhamma. In the Suttānta, the five 'aggregates' are classified partially and not fully. In the Abhidhamma they are classified fully by the methods of the Suttānta-classification, Abhidhamma-classification, and catechism."

46 Jaini, *Abhidharmadīpa*, pp. 47-48, quotes the Sautrāntika Yaśomitra as saying that the Sarvāstivādins' seven *abhidharma* treatises were not the word of the Buddha, but only that of his followers. He gives as his argument that each of the treatises has its author's name appended to it, so how could they be the word of the Buddha? He claimed that the name *abhidharma* was given to a certain type of sūtra, "dealing with the determination of meanings and characteristics of *dharmas*." The Sarvāstivādins, while acknowledging that their seven treatises did have their authors'

names attached to them, they still could be considered the "word of Buddha" since they had nothing in them that was not contained in the sūtras, and so their authors were more like editors than authors.

47 P. Maung Tin, *The Expositor*, vol. 1, pp. 16ff.; also, Wilhelm Geiger, *Pali Literature and Language* (New Delhi: Oriental Books Reprint Corp., 1978), p. 47 n.

48 A. K. Warder, *Indian Buddhism*, pp. 88-89.

49 For example, by Jaini, *Abhidharmadīpa*, pp. 28-29.

50 William Dwight Whitney, *Sanskrit Grammar*, 2nd ed. (repr., Cambridge, Mass.: Harvard University Press, 1967), p. 35. Whitney estimates that the roots that have an authentic occurrence in the language at about eight or nine hundred, while the number hypothesized by Indian grammarians was about two thousand or more. Their philosophy demanded that all nouns be reducible to verb roots.

51 The criteria used by the different schools for deciding which texts were the word of the Buddha and which were not were quite various. The way in which these criteria affected which texts were to be included in the canon is discussed by Jaini, in *Abhidharmadīpa*, pp. 22-29, and, with a different emphasis, by Étienne Lamotte in "La critique d'authenticité dans le bouddhisme," in *India Antiqua: A Volume of Oriental Studies Presented by His Friends and Pupils to Jean Philippe Vogel, C. I. E., on the Occasion of the Fiftieth Anniversary of His Doctorate* (Leyden: E. J. Brill, 1947), pp. 213-222.

52 *Aṅguttara-nikāya* 4.163.

53 P. Maung Tin, *The Expositor*, vol. 1, pp. 5ff.

54 Raj Bali Pandey, *Indian Palaeography* (Benares: Motilal Banarasi Das, 1952), pp. 15-16.

55 Oldenberg, *Dīpavaṃsa*, Chap. 20, verses 20-21, pp. 103, 211.

56 Winternitz, *A History of Indian Literature*, vol. 2, p. 27; Burrow, *The Sanskrit Language*, p. 14.

57 Even textually conservative schools liked to compare the Buddha's teachings to the different dialects a multilingual teacher could adopt when addressing students from different countries. Bu-dön wrote in his history of Buddhism that at the time of Aśoka, about a hundred and sixty years after the Buddha's death, the monks were "reading the word of the Buddha" in four different languages—Sanskrit, Prakrit, Apabhramsa, and "Paiśāci." Some have believed that this last was Pali, but Bagchi, "Fundamental Problems," examines the evidence and finds it unconvincing. Renou, in *L'Inde Classique* (Paris: Imprimerie Nationale, 1953), vol. 2, p. 325, notes the exaggeration found in the *Vimalaprabhā*, that the Buddhist texts had been written in ninety-six countries, in ninety-six different languages.

58 Lamotte, *Histoire*, pp. 614, 617-622, 632-633; Bagchi, "Fundamental Problems," pp. 2232-2233; Brough, *The Gāndhāri Dharmapada*, pp. 48ff.; Edgerton, *Buddhist Hybrid Sanskrit and Grammar and Dictionary*, vol. 1, pp. 1-9.

59 Brough, *The Gāndhāri Dharmapada*, pp. 45ff.; compare to *Dhammapada*, verse 113.

60 The disagreement between the Sarvāstivādins and the Mahāsaṃghikas over this story is detailed in Demiéville, ed., *Hōbōgirin*, in his article on *Butsugo*, p. 208.

61 J. J. Jones, trans., *The Mahāvastu* (London: Pali Text Society, 1949), vol. 1, p. 135.

62 *Visuddhimagga* 14.21, trans. Ñāṇamoli, pp. 486-487.

63 Buddhadatta Thero, ed., *Sammoha-vinodanī Abhidhamma-piṭake Vibhaṅga-aṭṭhakathā* (London: Pali Text Society, 1923), pp. 387-388.

64 Étienne Lamotte, "Passions and Impregnations of the Passions in Buddhism," in L. Cousins et al., eds., *Buddhist Studies in Honour of I. B. Horner* (Dordrecht: D. Reidel, 1974), pp. 94-97.

65 Oldenberg, *Dīpavaṃsa*, Chap. 5, verses 32-38, pp. 36, 40-41.

66 Jiryo Masuda, "Origin and Doctrines of Early Indian Buddhist Schools: A Translation of the Hsüan-chwang Version of Vasumitra's Treatise," *Asia Major* 2 (1925): 1-78; Andre Bareau, "Trois traités sur les sectes bouddhiques attribués à Vasumitra, Bhavya et Vinītadeva," *Journal Asiatique* 242 (1954): 167-220 and 229-266. For other early sectarian disputes, see Bareau's *Les sectes bouddhiques du Petit Véhicule* (Saigon: École française d'Extrême-Orient, 1955); Paul Demiéville, "L'origine des sectes bouddhiques d'après Paramārtha," in his *Choix d'études bouddhiques* (Leiden: E. J. Brill, 1973), pp. 113-116; A. C. Taylor, ed., *Kathāvatthu* (London: Pali Text Society, 1894-97); Shwe Zan Aung and Caroline A. F. Rhys Davids, trans., *Points of Controversy* (London: Pali Text Society, 1915); Nalinaksha Dutt, *Buddhist Sects in India* (Calcutta: Firma K. L. Mukhopadhyay, 1970); Charles Prebish and Janice Nattier, "Mahāsāṃghika Origins: The Beginnings of Buddhist Sectarianism," *History of Religions* 16 (1977): 237-272.

67 Lamotte, "La critique d'interprétation," pp. 148, 172, 356.

68 Lamotte, *Le traité*, vol. 2, p. 1074.

69 Jaini, *Abhidharmadīpa*, p. 47.

70 Lamotte, "Passions and Impregnations," p. 97; Dutt, *Buddhist Sects in India*, p. 97.

71 Demiéville, *Hōbōgirin*, p. 217.

72 Étienne Lamotte has examined this passage in detail in *Le traité*, vol. 1, pp. 30-31.

73 *Guide through the Abhidhamma-Piṭaka* (Kandy: Buddhist Publications Society, 1971), p. 88.

74 Y. Karunadasa, *Buddhist Analysis of Matter* (Colombo: Department of Cultural Affairs, 1967), p. 6.

75 Translated by Edouard Chavannes, *Cinq cent contes et apologues: extraits du tripiṭaka chinois* (Paris: Ernest Leroux, 1911), vol. 2, pp. 150ff.

76 Chavannes, *Cinq cent contes et apologues*, vol. 2, p. 152.

77 *Ussada*: "dominance" or "extrusiveness" of one element over others in a group; Karunadasa, *Buddhist Analysis of Matter*, p. 27.

78 The lists of *dharma* in Vaibhāṣika sources in Akira Hirakawa, *Index to the Abhidharmakośa* (Tokyo: Daizo Shuppan Kabushiki Kaisha, 1973), vol. 1, pp. xii-xiv, and the Theravāda *abhidhamma* lists give no indication that gross objects, like trees or tables, were included in the lists of *dharma*, as is done in Tibetan Gelukpa presentations, where they would be classed as "objects of touch."

79 The Tibetan Gelukpas, however, maintain that in the system of the "Sautrāntikas Following Reasoning," that is, those who follow the system of Dignāga and Dharmakīrti, a pot, for example, is an ultimate truth, and that the "meaning generality of pot"—or pot's generic image—is a conventional truth, the point being that the pot itself is the plain, unmediated, particular, raw object (and so an ultimate thing, in and of itself), and the conceptualization of the pot, which interprets it and links it to an imagined image, is a kind of imaginary thing, but is nevertheless the commonality that is shared among all those who understand what a pot is, and so is the "conventional truth."

80 Nalinaksha Dutt, *Buddhist Sects in India*, p. 162.

81 Vilhelm Trenckner, ed., *The Milindapañho* (London: Royal Asiatic Society, 1928), pp. 27, 160; in *sūtra*, the simile is in *Saṃyutta-Nikāya*, ed. Léon Feer (London: Pali Text Society, 1884), vol. 1, p. 135.

82 Shotaro Iida, "An Introduction to Svātantrika-Mādhyamika" (Ph.D. dissertation, University of Wisconsin, 1968), pp. 264-265.

83 F. L. Woodward and E. M. Hare, *The Book of Gradual Sayings (Aṅguttara-nikāya)* (London: Pali Text Society, 1932), vol. 1, pp. 14-15.

84 Max Walleser, ed., *Manoratha-pūraṇī: Buddhaghosa's Commentary on the Aṅguttara-nikāya* (London: Pali Text Society, 1973), vol. 1, pp. 94-95.

85 Shwe Zan Aung and Caroline Rhys Davids, *Points of Controversy (Kathāvatthu)* (London: Pali Text Society, 1915), p. 8ff.; the terms *saccam* and *paramattha* are discussed in their appendix.

86 Nalinaksha Dutt, *Three Principal Schools of Buddhism* (Calcutta: C. O. Book Agency, 1939), pp. 58ff.

87 Shwe Zan Aung and Caroline Rhys Davids, *Points of Controversy (Kathāvatthu)*, p. 63 and note.

88 Nyanatiloka, *Guide through the Abhidhamma-Piṭaka*, pp. 2-3, which view is elaborated by Ledi Sadaw, "Some Points in Buddhist Doctrine," *Journal of the Pali Text Society* 7 (1914): 115-163, who sees the use of the term "person" as peculiar to the sūtras.

89 Louis de La Vallée Poussin, "Documents d'Abhidharma: Les deux, les quatre, les trois vérités," *Mélanges chinois et bouddhiques* 5 (1937): 170.

90 Theodor Stcherbatsky, *Buddhist Logic* (repr., New York: Dover, 1962), vol. 1, p. 70.

91 In this school and other classical Indian Buddhist schools, as well as in Theravāda, conventionally existent things, although devalued in some sense, are nevertheless "objects of knowledge" (*jñeya*); see Padmanabh S. Jaini, "The Vaibhāṣika Theory of Words and Meanings," *Bulletin of the School of Oriental Studies* 22 (1959): 101.

92 Paul M. Williams, "On the Abhidharma Ontology," *Journal of Indian Philosophy* 9 (1980): 239.

93 La Vallée Poussin, "Les deux, les quatre, les trois vérités," p. 170.

94 La Vallée Poussin, "Les deux, les quatre, les trois vérités," pp. 153-164; Iida, "An Introduction to Svātantrika-Mādhyamika," pp. 263-264, translates a passage from the *Mahāvibhāṣā* that states the same positions.

95 In his note to this, La Vallée Poussin says that Vasumitra reported that the Bahuśrutīyas asserted that the five teachings of the Buddha—impermanence, suffering, emptiness, selflessness, and nirvāṇa—were supramundane, and that the other teachings were mundane. This listing of teachings resembles a selection of these same attributes of the four noble truths.

96 La Vallée Poussin, "Les deux, les quatre, les trois vérités," pp. 170ff.

97 K. N. Jayatilleke, *Early Buddhist Theory of Knowledge* (London: George Allen & Unwin, 1963), pp. 367-368, which discusses *Kathāvatthu* 310 on the nature of *sammuti-ñānam.*

98 Charles Willemen, trans., *The Essence of Metaphysics: Abhidharmahṛdaya* (Brussels: L'institut belge des hautes études bouddiques, 1975); this text was written by Dharmaśrī of the Gandhāra branch of the Vaibhāṣika School. On pp. 86ff., he explains that the only category of knowledge (*jñāna*) that does not have the sixteen attributes of the four truths is *saṃvṛti-satya.* LVP, Chap. 7, pp. 15, 27-28, deals with *jñāna* and its ten varieties, as well as the relationship between the cognition of the two truths and the cognition of the sixteen attributes of the four truths.

99 The Vaibhāṣikas held that 1) "partless particles"—that is, particles that could not be further divided, 2) partless moments of consciousness—"quanta" of consciousness, and 3) unconditioned phenomena constituted the categories of ultimates, but by the peculiar wording of the criterion in the *Abhidharmakośa,* we can infer that anything whose name remained the same after being broken apart was an ultimate, as with space (*ākāśa*), every portion of which is also space. Therefore, form (*rūpa*), taken to mean either a gross form or a single "form" particle, could also be considered an ultimate.

100 According to A. K. Warder, *Indian Buddhism,* p. 344, this was not the Vasumitra who wrote the compendium of early schools' doctrines, but the Sarvāstivāda sectarian who wrote the last of the seven of the Sarvāstivādins' basic *abhidharma* treatises, the *Prakaraṇa-pada.* The quote is from La Vallée Poussin, "Les deux, les quatre, les trois vérités," p. 177.

101 La Vallée Poussin, "Les deux, les quatre, les trois vérités," pp. 177-178.

102 Padmanabh S. Jaini, *Abhidharmadīpa,* p. 263.

103 Listed in Hirakawa, *Index,* vol. 1, pp. xii-xiv.

104 Jaini, "The Vaibhāṣika Theory," p. 95.

105 Jaini, "The Vaibhāṣika Theory," p. 96, translating the *Abhidharmadīpavṛtti.*

106 Jaini, "The Vaibhāṣika Theory," p. 96, translating the *Abhidharmakośa-vyākhyā.*

107 LVP, Chap. 2, verse 47; discussed in Jaini, "The Vaibhāṣika Theory," p. 97.

108 LVP, Chap. 2, verse 239; discussed in Jaini, "The Vaibhāṣika Theory," pp. 100-101.

109 Jaini, "The Vaibhāṣika Theory," p. 107.

110 Patañjali, *Mahābhāṣya* 1.6.16; and *Mīmāṃsaka-sūtra* 1.1.5, in Jaimini, *Mīmāṃsādarśane,* Ānandāśrama Sanskrit Series, vol. 1 (Poona: Ānandāśrama mudramālya, 1929), p. 23—*autpattikas tu śabdayārthena sambandhas . . .*

111 Biardeau, *Théorie de la connaissance et philosophie,* pp. 155-156.

112 Theodor Stcherbatsky, *The Central Conception of Buddhism and the Meaning of the Word "Dharma"* (Calcutta: S. Gupta, 1961), p. 24 n.; Jaini, "The Vaibhāṣika Theory," p. 107; Biardeau, *Théorie de la connaissance et philosophie*, pp. 390-400.

113 LVP, Chap. 2, verse 47.

114 Lati Rinbochay and Elizabeth Napper, *Mind in Tibetan Buddhism* (Valois, N. Y.: Gabriel/Snow Lion, 1980), pp. 50-51.

115 Geshe Sopa and Jeffrey Hopkins, *Practice and Theory of Tibetan Buddhism* (New York: Grove Press, 1976), p. 81.

116 Sopa and Hopkins, *Practice and Theory of Tibetan Buddhism*, p. 81.

117 P5590, vol. 115, 124.2.1-124.2.2; LVP, Chap. 6, verse 4, pp. 139-140.

118 The commentary on this verse that Ngawang Belden gives in his work on the two truths, p. 6b, apparently interprets Vasubandhu's examples of "form . . . feelings, and so on" as referring to the five "aggregates" (Skt. *skandha*), although he does not exclude the other interpretation, for he also cites (p. 7a) Pūrṇavardhana's commentary, which glosses the examples as referring to the *caitasika* division of the ten *mahābhūmika*, such as *vedanā, saṃjñā, cetanā*, etc. Yaśomitra glosses Vasubandhu's examples to be of the *rūpa* and of the *caitasika*.

119 According to Bu-dön, *History of Buddhism*, p. 148, Pūrṇavardhana was the student of Sthiramati, who was the student of Vasubandhu. His commentary on the *Abhidharmakośa* is in the Tibetan canon. Ngawang Belden often cites it.

120 Translated by Louis de La Vallée Poussin, "Documents d'Abhidharma: La controverse du temps," *Mélanges chinois et bouddhiques* 5 (1937): 28. Saṃghabhadra's discussion of this subject is translated by La Vallée Poussin, "Documents d'Abhidharma," *Bulletin de l'École française d'Extrême-Orient* 30 (1930): 278ff.

121 La Vallée Poussin, "La controverse du temps," p. 28.

122 La Vallée Poussin, "La controverse du temps," p. 29; La Vallée Poussin, "Documents d'Abhidharma," p. 284.

123 Chakravarti, *Philosophy*, p. 47.

124 Chakravarti, *Philosophy*, p. 47; also quoted at length by Biardeau, *Théorie de la connaissance et philosophie*, pp. 57-58.

125 K. A. Subramania Iyer, ed. *Vākyapadīya, Kaṇḍa III* (Poona: Deccan College, 1963), 1.1.

126 Ngawang Belden on the two truths, p. 5a.

127 La Vallée Poussin, "Les deux, les quatre, les trois vérités," p. 174. In "Documents d'Abhidharma," p. 289, La Vallée Poussin speculates that Śrīlāta (or Śrīlabdha) was in fact the founder of a Sautrāntika subsect, but that Saṃghabhadra would not honor him with the title of "Sautrāntika."

128 La Vallée Poussin, "Les deux, les quatre, les trois vérités," p. 173.

129 These exceptions are given in the *Abhidharmakośa*, P5540, vol. 115, 118.2.2-118.2.3; LVP, Chap. 2, pp. 144ff.

130 Ngawang Belden, p. 7a, extrapolates the *Abhidharmakośa* explanation of atoms into the Form Realm. A clear explanation of the *Abhidharmakośa* system of the makeup of atoms in the different realms is given by the First Dalai Lama (dGe-'dun-grub), *mDzod tik thar lam gsal byed / Dam pa'i chos mngon pa'i mdzod kyi rnam par bshad pa thar lam gsal byed,* in vol. 3 of *The Collected Works of the First Dalai Lama Dge-'dun-grub-pa* (Gangtok: Dodrup Lama Sangye, 1979), p. 97a.

131 Karunadasa, *Buddhist Analysis of Matter,* p. 143; LVP, Chap. 2, p. 144, note 3.

132 Ngawang Belden, p. 5a: "Water . . . [is an example of] that which is mentally destroyed," and quoting Pūrṇavardhana: "Those [conventional things] which are mentally destroyed are such things as water, for it is impossible to separate out such things as the taste of water from it, for instance, through physically breaking it up." Ngawang Belden, p. 6a, also says, "Although the eight substances in a minute particle of water cannot be individually separated one from another [that is, physically isolated], the mind can separate water into its individual components such as water and taste."

133 Thus, the *Abhidharmakośa* does not admit that the fundamental elements (that is, *mahābhūta*) have the quality of visibility, and so concludes that saying that they can be seen is only a "worldly expression" (*lokasaṃjñā*) (LVP, Chap. 1, p. 23, discussed by Karunadasa, *Buddhist Analysis of Matter,* p. 29). Some held also that the smallest particle did not have "shape" for the same reason, as Ngawang Belden explains, p. 13a.

134 Karunadasa, *Buddhist Analysis of Matter,* p. 143; LVP, Chap. 1, pp. 24-25.

135 LVP, Chap. 11, p. 143, and Yaśomitra, I, pp. 34ff., and Karunadasa, *Buddhist Analysis of Matter,* pp. 148-149.

136 The Sautrāntikas' opponents, the Cittamātrins, reasoned that, "If, as the Sautrāntikas say, the atoms 'are extended,' . . . they can be divided and consequently do not substantially exist," Karunadasa, *Buddhist Analysis of Matter,* p. 149, discussing Hsüan Tsang's *Vijñaptimātratāsiddhi,* trans. Louis de La Vallée Poussin, *La Siddhi de Hiuan-tsang* (Paris: Paul Geuthner, 1928), vol. 1, pp. 40-41.

137 La Vallée Poussin, "La controverse du temps," p. 29.

138 Ngawang Belden on the two truths, p. 8a.

139 La Vallée Poussin, "Documents d'Abhidharma," p. 298.

140 That these were held to be synonymous is clear from Saṃghabhadra's remarks following in the text on the nature of space and of nirvāṇa. In addition, Gelukpa sources say that they are synonymous; see Sopa and Hopkins, *Practice and Theory of Tibetan Buddhism,* p. 71.

141 However, *bhāva* and *sat* apparently had different connotations even in the Vaibhāṣika School, where they were held to be "mutually inclusive" (*ekārtha*) terms. Saṃghabhadra defines *sat* as "that which produces an awareness (*buddhi*) that corresponds to an object (*viṣaya*)." In La Vallée Poussin, "Les deux, les quatre, les trois vérités," p. 27, Saṃghabhadra notes that the "Dārṣṭāntikas" (=Sautrāntikas) do not agree with this definition of *sat* since they hold that there are "awarenesses [produced] by a nonexistent object" (*asadviṣaya buddhiḥ*). In the Tibetan Gelukpa monastic texts, which inherited a system of definitions based on Dignāga and Dharmakīrti, *sat* (Tib. *yod pa*) is defined as "that which is established by valid cognition

(*pramāṇa*) [Tib. *tshad mas grub pa*]"; see Purbujok (Phur-bu-lcog Byams-pa rgya-mtsho), *Tshad ma'i gzhung don 'byed pa'i bsdus grwa'i rnam par bshad pa rigs lam 'phrul gyi lde mig* (Buxa, 1965), p. 56, line 6. The definitions of *sat*, therefore, are concerned with the fact that they are apprehended by the mind. Purbujok explains the definition of *bhāva* (Tib. *dgnos po*) differently, as "that which is capable of performing a function [Tib. *don byed nus pa*]." The term *bhāva*, therefore, connotes something that can function, and the term *sat* connotes something that is unmistakenly cognized. Hopkins, *Meditation on Emptiness*, p. 229, says, "according to . . . the Vaibhāṣikas, permanent phenomena [that is, *nitya*, for example, the three *asaṃskṛta*] are things [*bhava*] because, for instance, a space performs the function of allowing an object to be moved. The other systems of tenets . . . say that the presence or absence of another obstructive object is what allows or does not allow an object to be moved, not space itself, which is just a non-affirming negative."

142 La Vallée Poussin, "Documents d'Abhidharma," p. 266.

143 La Vallée Poussin, "Documents d'Abhidharma," p. 266.

144 La Vallée Poussin, "Documents d'Abhidharma," p. 277.

145 La Vallée Poussin, "Documents d'Abhidharma," pp. 277-278.

146 The distinction between *paryyudāsa-pratiṣedha* ("affirming negatives") and *prasajya-pratiṣedha* ("non-affirming negatives") was first made by the Mīmāṃsākas, according to Dhirendra Sharma, *The Differentiation Theory of Meaning in Indian Logic* (The Hague: Mouton, 1969), p. 34 n. They used them to refer to statements in Vedic ritual directions, and distinguished such statements that were absolute prohibitions from those that were merely prohibitions against failing to perform an act under specified conditions. Our text, however, uses these terms to refer to different sorts of phenomena, objects, and not primarily to refer to different sorts of statements. The three unconditioned phenomena—uncaused space, analytical cessations, and non-analytical cessations—are "non-affirming negative [phenomena]." That these terms should apply to both "propositions" and to phenomena can be understood by the fact that even single terms that name phenomena carry with them a predicate, such as "exists," even if it is not explicitly stated. In this view, all objects become, as it were, not isolated objects, but more like propositions occuring in some context, or on some locus.

147 Sopa and Hopkins, *Practice and Theory of Tibetan Buddhism*, pp. 75-76. They comment, "Vaibhāṣikas consider that there is always something affirmative about a negative because their system always deals with substantial entities." Ngawang Belden deals with this general topic on p. 8b. Here, he discusses the debate in the *Abhidharmakośa* on the nature of the *pratisaṃkhyānirodha* (P5591, vol. 115, 159.3.2-159.3.5; LVP, Chap. 2, p. 278).

148 Ngawang Belden, pp. 11a-13a. This debate on shape is in the *Abhidharmakośa* (P5591, vol. 115, 193.1.5-193.3.1; LVP, Chap. 4, pp. 9-10); Karunadasa, *Buddhist Analysis of Matter*, pp. 49-50 and 70ff., and cites Yaśomitra, I, p. 26.

149 Ngawang Belden reports the Sautrāntika position while commenting on the *Abhidharmakośa* (LVP, Chap. 4, p. 9). The relationship of single particles and composites of particles to a perceiving consciousness figures into the debate between the Sautrāntikas and the Vaibhāṣikas over whether or not one particle could rightly be called a "source" (*āyatana*) of a consciousness, treated in *Abhidharmakośa* (P5591,

vol. 115, 131.4.1ff.; LVP, Chap. 1, p. 39) and by Ngawang Belden on the two truths, p. 10b, who also has a debate on the positions of the various schools on whether or not each of the minute particles in a composite appears to a sense consciousness.

150 Ngawang Belden on the two truths, pp. 16a-17a.

151 For a hint at some of the complexity of positions taken in these debates, see Sopa and Hopkins, *Practice and Theory of Tibetan Buddhism*, especially pp. 107-110. However, Ngawang Belden's presentation of these positions differs with that of Sopa and Hopkins in that Ngawang Belden says that the Vaibhāṣikas claimed that subject and object exist simultaneously, while Sopa and Hopkins, p. 108, state that, "only in the Cittamātra and Yogācāra-Svātantrika systems do object and subject exist simultaneously."

152 Lokesh Chandra, *Materials for a History of Tibetan Literature*, Śata-piṭaka Series, vol. 29, part 2 (New Delhi: International Academy of Indian Culture, 1963), pp. 10-13, 282-284, and from his *Eminent Tibetan Polymaths of Mongolia*, Śata-piṭaka Series, vol. 16 (New Delhi: International Academy of Indian Culture, 1961), pp. 22-24, 50-52.

153 See Robert James Miller, *Monasteries and Culture Change in Inner Mongolia* (Wiesbaden: Otto Harrassowitz, 1959), pp. 43-47, 53, for an explanation and list of monastic and academic ranks in Mongolia.

154 Ngawang Belden is also known as Belden Chöjay (dPal-ldan Chos-rje) or Khalka Chöjay (Khal-ka Chos-rje); see Andrei Ivanovich Vostrikov, "Some Corrections and Critical Remarks on Dr. Johan van Manem's Contribution to the Bibliography of Tibet," *Bulletin of the School of Oriental Studies* 8 (1935): 73 n.

155 *Grub mtha'i bzhi'i lugs kyi kun rdzob dang don dam pa'i don rnam par bshad pa legs bshad dpyid kyi dpal mo'i glu dbyangs*. The translation was done from the edition printed by Lama Guru Deva (New Delhi, 1972), which was reproduced from a copy xylographed from the blocks at the State Library in Ulan Bataar.

156 The text begins with an invocation of Mañjuśrī, the manifestation of the wisdom of the Buddhas. By marking syllables in the text, Ngawang Belden spells out the name of his own teacher, Ngawang Keydrup (Ngag-dbang mKhas-grub). See Chandra, *Materials for a History of Tibetan Literature*, pp. 10-11, and his *Eminent Tibetan Polymaths*, pp. 22-23; also, Georg Huth, *Geschichte des Buddhismus in der Mongolei* (Strassburg: Karl J. Trübner, 1896), vol. 1, pp. 240ff. In 1835, at the time this book was written, Ngawang Keydrup was the chief spiritual authority in Urga, the Kenchen (*mkhan-chen*), and Ngawang Belden was holding a post just below him, that of Chöjay (*chos-rje*).

157 Ngawang Belden invokes the teachers in his spiritual lineage, either by name or metaphor, invoking a mythology shared with Hindu India. In this paragraph, Śākyamuni Buddha, called the "King of Subduers," is characterized in a way similar to Indra.

158 Here, a Buddha is reckoned to have two bodies—his Form Body (*rūpa kāya*) and his Truth Body (*dharma kāya*). One gains a Form Body primarily by cultivating the means to enlightenment—which consist of techniques for developing compassion and for controlling appearances—that is, phenomena identified as conventional truths. One gains a Truth Body by cultivating the wisdom that directly realizes the emptiness of things' inherent existence, that is to say, that realizes ultimate truth. A

Buddha has thirty-two major and eighty minor marks, which are features of his Form Body and that mark him as a Buddha. The Truth Body is here placed "along the collected immortals' broad path," which is to say the pathway of the gods, that is, the sky, because of ultimate truth's high, deathless clarity.

159 Maitreya, the Buddha who will come some time in the future, is the "regent" of Śākyamuni (the "Conqueror") because he is to act in Śākyamuni's absence. The pairs here of Maitreya and Mañjuśrī, as well as of Nāgārjuna and Asaṅga, also refer to lineages of teachings about the "vast"—conventional truths—and the "profound"—ultimate truths.

160 The group of three authors mentioned here are Śāntarakṣita, author of the *Ornament for the Middle Way (Madhyamakālaṃkāra)*, Jñānagarbha, author of the *Differentiation of the Two Truths (Satyadvaya Vibhaṅga)*, and Kamalaśīla, author of the *Illumination of the Middle Way (Madhyamakālokā)*. The "one from the island of Suvarṇa" (that is, Sumatra) was Atīśa's teacher of Cittamātra tenets, who was named either Dharmakīrti or Dharmapāla; see Alaka Chattopadhyaya, *Atīśa and Tibet* (Calcutta: Indian Studies Past and Present, 1967), pp. 84-95.

161 Mañjuśrī of the Tathāgata lineage, Avalokiteśvara of the Lotus lineage, and Vajrapāṇi of the Vajra lineage are the protectors of the three lineages; Atīśa's main Tibetan disciple was Dromdön ('Brom-ston rGyal-ba'i 'Byung-gnas, 1003-1063), founder of the Kadampa sect, a branch of which was a precursor of the Gelukpa sect.

162 Tsongkhapa (Tsong-kha-pa, 1357-1419), founder of the Gelukpa sect, is compared in this verse to the second, fourth, and sixth incarnations of Viṣṇu.

163 "Those who wear the golden crown" refers to the "yellow hats" or Gelukpas. The two main disciples of Tsongkhapa were Gyaltsap (rGyal-mtshap Dar-ma-rin-chen, 1364-1462) and Keydrup (mKhas-grub dGe-legs dPal-bzang, 1385-1483). The imagery in this passage is very unusual—whereas Śākyamuni is reckoned as the ninth incarnation of Viṣṇu, Buddhists ordinarily count Maitreya as the tenth, but here, Śākyamuni's teachings are reckoned as the tenth incarnation.

164 Jamyang Shayba ('Jam-dbyangs bzhad-pa'i rdo-rje, 1648-1721) was the principal textbook writer of the Gomang college of Drepung Monastery in Lhasa. His name literally means "Vajra at whom Mañjuśrī smiled." The imagery in this verse again recalls Indra.

165 Probably Ngawang Belden's teacher Ngawang Keydrup.

166 The beryl's eight facets are perhaps the two truths in the four tenet systems.

167 P6016, vol. 153, 38.1.1-38.1.3.

168 P5224, vol. 95, 9.2.5.

169 The sūtra is titled *'Phags pa de kho na nyid ting nge 'dzin nges par bstan pa'i mdo*, but there is no mention of it in the Peking, Tōhoku (see Hakuju Ui, *A Complete Catalogue of the Tibetan Buddhist Canons*), or Nanjio catalogs. However, it is quoted at longer length in Candrakīrti's *Madhyamakāvatāra*; see Louis de La Vallée Poussin, ed., *Madhyamakāvatāra par Candrakīrti* (St. Petersburg: Imprimerie de l'Académie impériale des sciences, 1912), pp. 175-177. Perhaps it is related to the *Pitāputrasamāgama-sūtra*, from which Candrakīrti in the *Madhyamakāvatāra*, p. 70, takes an almost identical quote.

170 P5224, vol. 95, 9.2.6-7; Chap. 24, verses 10-11.

171 P5261, vol. 98, 103.1.5-103.1.6; Chap. 6, verse 4.

172 This work is not listed in P, but is Tōh 3881.

173 Tsongkhapa, *In Praise of Dependent-Arising*, P6016, vol. 153, 38.1.2-38.1.3.

174 "Even" is said here because liberation from cyclic existence is a lower goal than omniscience; the former goal it is possible to attain through the "hearer vehicle" (*Śrāvakayāna*) and the "solitary-realizer vehicle" (*Pratyekabuddhayāna*), but the latter is only possible with the attainment of Buddhahood, which is the fruit of the "Bodhisattva vehicle" (*Bodhisattvayāna*). Tsongkhapa maintained that only the Prāsaṅgikas asserted that Hearers and Solitary Realizers cognized the highest reality, just as those in the Bodhisattva Vehicle did; see Jeffrey Hopkins, trans., *Tantra in Tibet: The Great Exposition of Secret Mantra by Tsong-ka-pa* (London: George Allen & Unwin, 1977), p. 40.

175 P795, vols. 31-32.

176 P5255, vol. 96, 4.1.4.

177 P5709, vol. 130, 79.4.2-3.

178 Killing one's mother, father, or an Arhat, causing the blood to flow with evil intent from the body of a Buddha, and causing dissension in the spiritual community.

179 Tsongkhapa, *Ocean of Reasoning, Explanation of (Nāgārjuna's) "Treatise on the Middle Way" (dbU ma rtsa ba'i tshig le'ur byas pa shes rab ces bya ba'i rnam bshad rigs pa'i rgya mtsho)* (Varanasi: Pleasure of Elegant Sayings Printing Press, 1973), pp. 10-12.

180 P5246, vol. 95, 131.1.1.

181 The "proponents of true existence" (*dngos smra ba* or *dngos po bden par grub par smra ba*) refers to the Indian Buddhist schools besides the Mādhyamika—the Vaibhāṣika, the Sautrāntika, and the Cittamātra.

182 Śrāvaka (literally, "hearer") here does not refer to the spiritual lineage, as in the three "vehicles" of *Śrāvakayāna*, *Pratyekabuddhayāna*, and *Bodhisattvayāna*, but rather refers to a sectarian division that Ngawang Belden is choosing to make within the Indian Buddhist schools, using the word to refer to the Vaibhāṣika (or Sarvāstivāda) School and the Sautrāntika.

183 P5590, vol. 115, 124.2.1-124.2.2; LVP, Chap. 6, verse 4, pp. 139-140.

184 P5591, vol. 115, 243.4.8ff.; LVP, Chap. 6, p. 141.

185 P5590, vol. 115, 124.2.1-124.2.2; LVP, Chap. 6, verse 4, pp. 139-140.

186 P5591, vol. 115, 243.4.8ff.; LVP, Chap. 6, p. 141.

187 *Grub mtha'i rnam bshad rang gzhan grub mtha' kun dang zab don mchog tu gsal ba kun bzang zhing gi nyi ma lung rigs rgya mtsho skye dgu'i re ba kun skyong*, in *The Collected Works of 'Jam-dbyaṅs-bźad-pa'i-rdo-rje, Reproduced from Prints from the Bkra-śis-'khyil Blocks*, vol. 14 (New Delhi: Ngawang Gelek Demo, 1973).

188 *Tshad ma rigs rgyan*, which is *Tshad ma'i bstan bcos chen po rigs pa'i rgyan*. A distinction between *rdzas su yod pa* and *rdzas yod* does not ordinarily exist, both phrases

being used as equivalent to translate the Sanskrit *dravya-sat*. Any distinction is ad hoc.

189 P5594, vol. 118, 17.2.2-4.

190 *Abhidharmakośa-vyākhyā-sphuṭārtha*, P5593, vol. 116, 274.2.1-2; LVP, Chap. 6, p. 140.

191 *Mūlamadhyamakavṛtti-prasannapadā*, P5260, vol. 98; these three etymologies of *saṃvṛti* are given in Louis de La Vallée Poussin, ed., *Mūlamadhyamakakārikās de Nāgārjuna avec la Prasannapadā commentaire de Candrakīrti* (St. Petersburg: Imprimerie de l'Académie impériale des sciences, 1903-1913), p. 492.

192 Chintamani Shastri Thatte and F. Kielhorn, eds., *Amarakośa, with the Commentary of Maheśvara* (Bombay: Government Central Book Depot, 1877), pp. 39-40, verse 22, and p. 321, verse 153 (*satyam*); p. 28, verse 22 (*saṃvartaḥ*).

193 P5591, vol. 115, 243.5.2; LVP, Chap. 6, p. 141.

194 P5591, vol. 115, 242.5.3-4; LVP, Chap. 6, p. 141.

195 P5594, vol. 118, 17.2.5-6.

196 Not found in P.

197 P5590, vol. 115, 118.2.2-3; LVP, Chap. 2, pp. 144ff.

198 This verse is not in the *Abhidharmakośa*, but is constructed on the model of the previous verse.

199 *Pramāṇavārttika*, P5709, vol. 130, 88.3.5-6.

200 P5717(b), vol. 130, 217.1.1.

201 Because Devendrabuddhi was a student of Dharmakīrti and was therefore not a Vaibhāṣika, but a Sautrāntika.

202 Perhaps this text is Keydrup's *sDe bdun dka' 'grel yid kyi mun sel.*

203 *Grub mtha'i rnam bshad rang gzhan grub mtha' kun dang zab don mchog tu gsal ba*, in *The Collected Works of 'Jam-dbyaṅs-bźad-pa'i-rdo-rje*, vol. 14, p. 322, lines 4ff.

204 P5591, vol. 115, 159.3.2-5; La Vallée Poussin (LVP, Chap. 2, p. 278) says the "root text" referred to here is Kātyāyanīputra's *Jñānaprasthāna*.

205 This title is volume 12 of *The Collected Works of 'Jam-dbyaṅs-bźad-pa'i-rdo-rje, Reproduced from Prints from the Bkra-śis-'khyil Blocks* (New Delhi: Ngawang Gelek Demo, 1973).

206 P5591, vol. 115, 159.3.5-8; LVP, Chap. 2, pp. 278-279. La Vallée Poussin says the last example means, "when an untimely death interrupts one's existence, there is an *apratisaṃkhyā-nirodha* of the *dharma* which would have been born in the course of that existence if it had continued."

207 P5867, vol. 146, 115.3.6.

208 P5868, vol. 146, 130.5.3-5.

209 P5590, vol. 115, 117.3.3; LVP, Chap. 1, p. 35 (verse 20, a-b) and pp. 37-38.

210 P5592, vol. 108, 20.4.2; also, Ram Chandra Pandeya, ed., *Madhānta-vibhāga-śāstra* (Delhi: Motilal Banarsidass, 1971), pt. 3, verse 17a, p. 108; and P5562, vol. 113, 291.1.2ff.

211 P5261, vol. 98, 97.5.8.

212 P5591, vol. 115, 131.3.5; LVP, Chap. 1, p. 38.

213 P5591, vol. 115, 131.3.5-6.

214 P5591, vol. 115, 131.3.6.

215 P5591, vol. 115, 131.3.6-7. The third of the Cittamātrins' *triskandha*, according to Edgerton, *Buddhist Hybrid Sanskrit Grammar and Dictionary*, vol. 2, p. 608, is "requesting teaching from a Buddha."

216 P5591, vol. 115, 131.3.8-4.1; LVP, Chap. 1, pp. 38-39.

217 P5591, vol. 115, 131.4.1; LVP, Chap. 1, p. 39.

218 P5591, vol. 115, 131.4.1-2; LVP, Chap. 1, p. 39.

219 P5591, vol. 115, 131.4.2-5; LVP, Chap. 1, p. 39.

220 P5591, vol. 115, 193.1.5.-2.2; LVP, Chap. 4, p. 9.

221 P5591, vol. 115, 193.2.2-3; LVP, Chap. 4, pp. 9-10.

222 P5591, vol. 115, 193.2.3-5; LVP, Chap. 4, p. 10.

223 P5591, vol. 115, 193.2.5-193.3.1; LVP, Chap. 4, p. 10.

224 *Legs bshad gser gyi phreng ba, shes rab kyi pha rol tu phyin pa'i man ngag gi bstan bcos mngon par rtogs pai rgyan 'grel pa dang bcas pa'i rgya cher bshad pa*; P6150, vol. 154.

225 Again, perhaps this text is Keydrup's *sDe bdun dka' 'grel yid kyi mun sel.*

226 P5284, vol. 101, 1.2.1-2.

227 P5285, vol. 101, 3.5.7-8.

228 Again, perhaps this text is Keydrup's *sDe bdun dka' 'grel yid kyi mun sel.*

229 P5590, vol. 115, 126.5.6.

230 P5272, vol. 99, 258.5.7.

231 *Byang chub sems pa'i spyod pa la 'jug pa'i rnam bshad rgyal sras 'jug ngos.*

232 It is not clear who the Ākāśadevas were—perhaps Śaivites? I have merely reconstructed their name from the Tibetan.

233 P5590, vol. 115, 125.4.7.

234 P5255, vol. 96, 10.1.7-8.

235 P5255, vol. 96, 88.5.3-5.

236 P5224, vol. 95, 7.3.4-5.

237 P5658, vol. 129, 181.2.2-4; also, Jeffrey Hopkins, *The Precious Garland*, p. 76.

238 P5246, vol. 95, 139.2.6.

239 P5255, vol. 96.

240 According to Geshe Yeshe Tupden's oral commentary on this text, these ten are: *1-6. khams gsum gyi mtshungs ldan dang mtshungs ldan ma yin pa; 7. 'dus ma byas kyi dge*

ba; 8. 'dus ma byas kyi lung ma bstan; 9-10. zag med kyi mtshungs ldan ma yin pa (gnyis).

241 P5591, vol. 115; in the chapter on *jñāna* probably, but I have not found it.

242 P5594, vol. 118; the general topic is discussed in the chapter on *prajñā.*

243 This quote is not in the Peking edition's *Sugatagrantamata-vibhaṅga-kārikā* (P5867, vol. 146) but it does occur as an embedded verse in Jetāri's commentary, *Sugatagrantamata-vibhaṅga-bhāṣya* (P5868, vol. 146, at 130.3.4-5), except that line two in the P version has *rdul phran* instead of Ngawang Belden's *phra rab.*

244 I have not located the source of this quote, although it is definitely not from the *Sugutagrantamatavibhaṅga Kārikā,* nor have I found it in *Jetāri's Bhāṣya.*

245 Sopa and Hopkins, *Practice and Theory of Tibetan Buddhism,* pp. 107-110, have more about this division of the Cittamātra tenet system and the doctrinal debates on this issue.

246 P5867, vol. 146, 130.3.7-4.1.

247 *Drang ba dang nges pa'i don rnam par phye ba'i bstan bcos legs bshad snying po,* P6142, vol. 153.

248 *Grub mtha'i rnam bshad rang gzhan grub mtha' kun dang zab don mchog tu gsal ba,* vol. 14 of his *Collected Works;* this passage, however, does not appear in his discussion of the two truths according to the system of the *Abhidharmakośa* at pp. 322ff. and pp. 360ff.

249 Jamyang Shayba, p. 69b.4ff; Ngawang Belden, *Annotations for Jamyang Shayba's* Great Exposition of Tenets (*Grub mtha' chen mo'i mchan 'grel dka' gnad mdud grol blo gsal gces nor*) (Sarnath: Pleasure of Elegant Sayings Printing Press, 1964), vol. *dbu,* p. 35b.1ff.

250 P5700, vol. 130, 3.1.4-5.

251 P5709, vol. 130, 91.4.5-6.

Index

Printed in the United States
by Baker & Taylor Publisher Services